THE REVELATION OF THE TRINITY OF GOD

GOD
† the FATHER
† he SON
† he HOLY SPIRIT

DR. SNOW

XULON PRESS

Table of Contents

Part One: God The Father

1. The Lord's Prayer And The Father In Heaven
   A. The Lord's Prayer To The Father In Heaven In Matthew 13
   B. The Lord's Prayer To The Heavenly Father In Luke 14
2. John The Baptist And The Trinity Of God
   A. Matthew's Testimony Of John The Baptist And The Trinity 16
   B. Mark's Testimony Of John The Baptist And The Trinity 17
   C. Luke's Testimony Of John The Baptist And The Trinity 18
3. The Transfiguration Of Jesus Christ With Moses And Elijah In
   Communication With His Heavenly Father.
   A. Matthew's Account Of The Transfiguration With Moses And
      Elijah With Jesus Christ And His Heavenly Father 22
   B. Mark's Account Of The Transfiguration With Moses And Elijah
      With Jesus Christ And His Heavenly Father.................23
   C. Luke's Account Of The Transfiguration With Moses And Elijah
      With Jesus Christ And His Heavenly Father.................25
4. Comparison Of Matthew, Mark, Luke, And John 26
5. The Holy Spirit Is The Father Of Jesus Christ 27
6. Luke 15 The Church Sheep Of Jesus Christ Planet Earth 100% 29
7. The Apostle John's Account Of Jesus Christ The Shepherd 32
8. The Father In Heaven Gives You The Holy Spirit 35
9. The Keys Of The Kingdom Of The Heavenly Father 37
10. The Kingdom Of Heaven Is Taken By The Force Of . The Father
    In Heaven 39
11. The Heavenly Kingdom Of The Heavenly Father Gives You 30, 60, And
    100 Times What You Sow In Harvest......................... 41
12 The Heavenly Father Gives The Kingdom And All Things To The Son .. 45

13. Matthew And The Kingdom Of Christ Equals The Kingdom Of God In Manifestation Now 47

Part Two: God The Son In Jesus Christ

1. Matthew's Account Of The Birth Of Jesus Christ 55
2. Three Sets Of 14 Generations Explained 58
3. Luke's Account Of The Birth Of Jesus Christ 60
4. Holidays Are Connected To God And Jesus Christ 66
5. Jesus Christ Is Born Savior Of The World 68
6. Three Men Visit Abraham 70
7. The Tradition Of The Christ Tree At Christmas Time Is True Because The Christ Tree Is The Christmas Tree 74
8. The Tradition Of The Christ Tree At Church During Christmas Is The Cross Of Calvary 78
9. Jesus Christ On The Cross Removed All Sin 100% 80
10. Jesus Christ Is The Creator Of All Humanity Because He Made Us 84

Part Three: God The Holy Spirit

1. The Holy Spirit Is God Creator Of Creation....................... 91
2. The Holy Spirit Is The Breath Of Life 93
3. The Holy Spirit In The Birth Of Jesus Christ 95
4. The Holy Spirit Makes Us Sons And Daughters Of God 97
5. The Holy Spirit Appears With The Father And The Son 99
6. The Holy Spirit Descends Upon The Christ Of God 101
7. John The Baptist Baptizes Jesus Christ In The Holy Spirit 103
8. The Holy Spirit Helps Jesus Christ Defeat The Devil 100% 105
9. The Holy Spirit Is Our Counselor, Teacher, And Helper 108
10. The Holy Spirit In The Book Of Romans......................... 110
11. The Holy Spirit In The Name Of Jesus Christ Has Already Done Away With All The Power Of Sin At The Cross Of Calvary 100 Percent, It Is Done. 117
12. The Holy Spirit Cleanses And Sanctifies Us Into Holiness More And More Many Times Continually................................. 120

Introduction To The Revelation Of The Trinity Of God

The Trinity of God is one of the greatest mysteries of the Holy Bible because the Holy Bible is a book that reveals the qualities and personality of God. The Trinity of God consists of three main personalities. The first main personality of the God Head in the Holy Bible is the Heavenly Father. The second main personality of the God Head is the Son revealed in the LORD Jesus Christ. The third main personality of the God Head is The Holy Spirit of God who lives inside of every Christian. Many Christians know about the Trinity of God. The Trinity of God is best recognized as God the Father, God the Son, and God the Holy Spirit. This book is written to explain the Trinity of God to both new Christians and also to Christians that have already grown in their personal relationship with God. It is with great expectation and high hopes that all Christians may learn and receive some new insight to who God is. It is also our objective to show Christians of all ages that they can come to know God better and grow into deeper levels of understanding of the Holy Spirit of God. Learning something new about the character and personality of God is always something exciting, great, and amazing. It is possible that the following pages may contain one or two new insights of spiritual understanding when it comes to the understanding and teaching of the Trinity of God.

GOD † he FATHER

PART ONE:

God The Father

1

A. THE LORD'S PRAYER TO THE FATHER IN MATTHEW

Matthew the Apostle of Jesus Christ shows the Heavenly Father speaking from the clouds of heaven. Matthew was a Tax Collector that Jesus Christ called to be one of His Twelve Apostles. The Apostle Matthew wrote the Book of Matthew that is the first book of the New Testament of The Holy Bible. The Gospel of Matthew is the most respected of the four Gospels when it comes to the Teaching of The Kingdom of God that actually is The Kingdom of The Heavenly Father. The Kingdom of Heaven is found in the Book of Matthew over 30 times. God the Father provides New Things for you every time you say The LORD's Prayer of The Heavenly Father. Matthew 6:8-13 says, " Be not ye therefore like unto them: because your Father knoweth what things ye have need of, before ye ask him. After this manner therefore pray ye: Our Father which art in heaven, Hallowed be thy name. Thy kingdom come, Thy will be done in earth, as it is in heaven. Give us this day our daily bread. And forgive us our debts, as we forgive our debtors. And lead us not into temptation, but deliver us from evil: For thine is the kingdom, and the power, and the glory, forever. Amen."(KJV 996)

Many passages in the Holy Bible refer to God as our Heavenly Father. Perhaps the most familiar of these passages is when Jesus Christ teaches his disciples to pray to their Father in Heaven giving them this Model of Prayer in Matthew Chapter 6. Here we see the exemplary relationship that God the Father has with His Son Jesus Christ. God the Father along with his Son Jesus Christ reveals this new side of his personality and has given us an example prayer to follow. Jesus Christ the Son of God reveals this new side of who GOD is. God will become God the Father to His disciples and to all Christians in the future forever. Therefore we are able to see clearly that God the Father sent his Son Jesus Christ to Planet Earth to teach us how to call God our Father in Heaven with this new name: Heavenly Father.

The LORD's Prayer in Matthew Chapter 6 is the LORD's Prayer that the Holy Spirit our LORD empowers us to pray. The LORD's Prayer is the Prayer that the LORD Jesus Christ taught us to pray to the Heavenly Father. The LORD

GOD Our Heavenly Father is the LORD to whom this prayer is addressed. This prayer is primarily given to us to commune directly to our Heavenly Father in The Kingdom Heaven. This prayer is the direct teaching of the LORD Jesus Christ in the New Testament. The LORD in the LORD's Prayer is the LORD GOD Our Heavenly Father. The LORD in the LORD's Prayer is The LORD Jesus Christ. The LORD in The LORD's Prayer is The Holy Spirit who is also LORD. So in Summary The LORD's Prayer is a prayer taught to us by The LORD Jesus Christ in the Empowerment of our LORD The Holy Spirit to pray to our LORD GOD OUR FATHER IN HEAVEN.

THE TRINITY IS LIKE THREE ONES

B. THE LORD'S PRAYER TO THE HEAVENLY FATHER IN THE BOOK OF LUKE

Luke shows how Jesus Christ taught his disciples to pray to God the Father in Heaven in Luke 11:1-10 that teaches, "And it came to pass, that, as he was praying in a certain place, when he ceased, one of his disciples said unto him, Lord, teach us to pray, as John also taught his disciples. And he said unto them, When ye pray, say, Our Father that art in heaven, Hallowed be thy name. Thy kingdom come. Thy will be done, as in heaven, so in earth. Give us day by day our daily bread. And forgive us our sins; for we also forgive every one that is indebted to us. And lead us not into temptation; but deliver us from evil. And he said unto them, Which of you shall have a friend, and shall go unto him at midnight, and say unto him, Friend, lend me three loaves; For a friend of mine in his journey is come to me, and I have nothing to set before him? And he from within shall answer and say, Trouble me not: the door is now shut, and my children are with me in bed; I cannot rise and give thee. I say unto you, Though he will not rise and give him, because he is his friend, yet because of his importunity he will rise and give him as many as he needeth. And I say unto you, Ask, and it shall be given you; seek, and ye shall find; knock, and it shall be opened unto you. For every one that asketh receiveth; and he that seeketh findeth; and to him that knocketh it shall be opened."(KJV 1074) Jesus Christ is God teaching us how to pray to God.

THREE CIRCLES OF THE TRINITY OF GOD

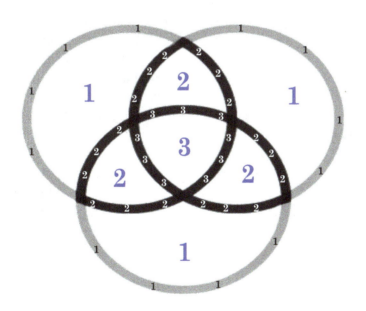

2

A. MATTHEW'S TESTIMONY OF JOHN THE BAPTIST AND THE TRINITY

Mathew records that he personally heard God the Heavenly Father audibly speak from the clouds of heaven as recorded in Matthew 3:11-17 that declares and maintains the words of John the Baptist, "I indeed baptize you with water unto repentance. but he that cometh after me is mightier than I, whose shoes I am not worthy to bear: he shall baptize you with the Holy Ghost, and with fire: Whose fan is in his hand, and he will throughly purge his floor, and gather his wheat into the garner; but he will burn up the chaff with unquenchable fire. Then cometh Jesus from Galilee to Jordan unto John, to be baptized of him. But John forbad him, saying, I have need to be baptized of thee, and comest thou to me? And Jesus answering said unto him, Suffer it to be so now: for thus it becometh us to fulfill all righteousness. Then he suffered him. And Jesus, when he was baptized, went up straightway out of the water: and, lo, the heavens were opened unto him, and he saw the Spirit of God descending like a dove, and lighting upon him: And lo a voice from heaven, saying, This is my beloved Son, in whom I am well pleased. Then was Jesus led up of the Spirit into the wilderness to be tempted of the devil. And when he had fasted forty days and forty nights, he was afterward an hungred."(KJV 992) Here in this passage GOD The Heavenly Father speaks about Jesus Christ His Son and says He is well pleased.

THREE TRIANGLES IN ONE TRIANGLE

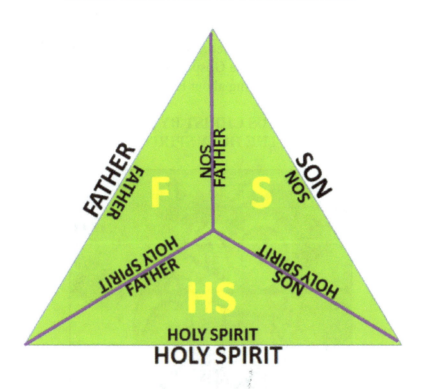

B. MARK'S TESTIMONY OF JOHN THE BAPTIST AND THE TRINITY

The Apostle John Mark is the writer of the Book of Mark. Even though John Mark was not one of the original 12 Apostles he was able to write the Gospel of Jesus Christ that is the main foundation of the three Synoptic Gospels of Matthew, Mark, and Luke. The term Synoptic Gospel comes the idea that both Matthew and Luke used the Gospel of Mark as a blue print in the writing of their account of the Life and Teachings of Jesus Christ. This is to say that without the Gospel of Mark, both the Gospel of Matthew and the Gospel of Luke if they would have been written could have been extensively different. The Word Gospel comes from the Greek word Evangelion that means "Good News". The Anglo Saxon word for Gospel is Godspell that also means "Good News". The Apostle John Mark also gives his account of The Heavenly Father Speaking from Heaven. Mark 1:6-12 testifies, "And John was clothed with camel's hair, and with a girdle of a skin about his loins; and he did eat locusts and wild honey; And preached, saying, There cometh one mightier than I after me, the latchet of whose shoes I am not worthy to stoop down and unloose. I indeed have baptized you with water: but he shall baptize you with the Holy Ghost. And it came to pass in those days, that Jesus came

17

from Nazareth of Galilee, and was baptized of John in Jordan. And straightway coming up out of the water, he saw the heavens opened, and the Spirit like a dove descending upon him: And there came a voice from heaven, saying, Thou art my beloved Son, in whom I am well pleased. And immediately the spirit driveth him into the wilderness."(KJV 1030) The Gospel of Mark is the original Gospel that recorded the Heavenly Father talking about His Son Jesus Christ.

THE BAPTISM OF JESUS CHRIST BY JOHN THE BAPTIST & THE HOLY SPIRIT

C. LUKE'S TESTIMONY OF JOHN THE BAPTIST AND THE TRINITY

The New Testament shows some examples of the Heavenly Father speaking from heaven. The four writers of the Gospels Matthew, Mark, Luke, and John each give accounts of having heard the Heavenly Father speak from Heaven. It was a time on planet Earth when in all actuality it was really Heaven on Earth! It was an amazing time because God the Father, God the Son, and God the Holy Spirit were all on planet Earth at the same time, at the same moment, and visible and audible at the same event.

The Apostle Luke was not one of the original 12 Apostles but he did write the Book of Luke that is one of the Gospels of Matthew, Mark, Luke, and John. Luke was also a companion and scribe of the Apostle Paul that wrote over half of the Books in the New Testament. So in a way since Luke was the scribe of the Apostle

Paul, Luke helped The Apostle Paul write down some of his ideas and teachings found in The New Testament.

The Gospel of Luke teaches about the Trinity of God. God the Father, God the Son, and God the Holy Spirit are all found in John the Baptist's Baptism of Jesus Christ in the Jordan River. The Apostle Luke testifies that he heard the Heavenly Father speak from heaven audibly as the Holy Spirit descended upon Jesus Christ in an appearance like a dove. Luke states and communicates that he personally heard the Heavenly Father speak from heaven in Luke 3:16-23 that records, " John answered, saying unto them all, I indeed baptize you with water; but one mightier than I cometh, the latchet of whose shoes I am not worthy to unloose: he shall baptize you with the Holy Ghost and with fire... Now when all the people were baptized, it came to pass, that Jesus also being baptized, and praying, the heaven was opened, And the Holy Ghost descended in a bodily shape like a dove upon him, and a voice came from heaven, that said, Thou art my beloved Son; in thee I am well pleased."(KJV 1060) The Holy voice speaking from heaven is the Holy Voice of The Heavenly Father.

THE TRINITY IS LIKE:
THE SON = THE CROSS

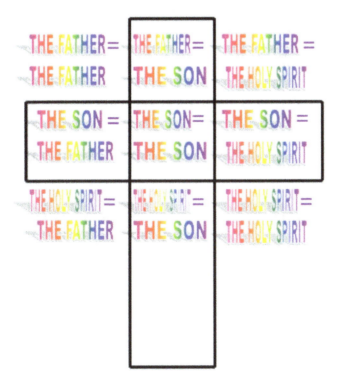

THE TRINITY IS LIKE:
THE ABC'S OF FAITH

1A is The Father = The Father

1B is The Father = Jesus Christ

1C is The Father = The Holy Spirit

THE TRINITY IS LIKE:

2A is Jesus Christ = The Father

2B is Jesus Christ = Jesus Christ

2C is Jesus Christ = The Holy Spirit

THE TRINITY IS LIKE:

3A is The Holy Spirit = The Father

3B is The Holy Spirit = Jesus Christ

3C is The Holy Spirit = The Holy Spirit

1A 1B 1C

2A 2B 2C

3A 3B 3C

THE TRINITY IS LIKE:
THE ABC'S OF FAITH

1A	1B	1C
2A	2B	2C
3A	3B	3C

3

A. MATTHEW'S ACCOUNT OF THE TRANSFIGURATION WITH MOSES AND ELIJAH WITH JESUS CHRIST AND HIS HEAVENLY FATHER

During the time when the transfiguration would happen Jesus Christ decides to take his top three apostles with him to a mountain to reveal Himself to them in a similar way as when God took Moses to a mountain to talk with him. Matthew 17:1-8 points out, "See the Son of man coming in his kingdom. And after six days Jesus taketh Peter, James, and John his brother, and bringeth them up into an high mountain apart, And was transfigured before them: and his face did shine as the sun, and his raiment was white as the light. And, behold, there appeared unto them Moses and Elias talking with him. Then answered Peter, and said unto Jesus, Lord, it is good for us to be here: if thou wilt, let us make here three tabernacles; one for thee, and one for Moses, and one for Elias. While he yet spake, behold, a bright cloud overshadowed them: and behold a voice out of the cloud, which said, This is my beloved Son, in whom I am well pleased; hear ye him. And when the disciples heard it, they fell on their face, and were sore afraid. And Jesus came and touched them, and said, Arise, and be not afraid. And when they had lifted up their eyes, they saw no man, save Jesus only. And as they came down from the mountain, Jesus charged them, saying, Tell the vision to no man, until the Son of man be risen again from the dead. And his disciples asked him, saying, Why then say the scribes that Elias must first come? And Jesus answered and said unto them, Elias truly shall first come, and restore all things. But I say to you, that Elias is come already."(KJV 1011) In this passage again the Heavenly Father speaks out of a cloud and says that He is pleased with his Son. This is the second time that the Apostle Matthew records the Heavenly Father speaking from Heaven.

THE TRANSFIGURATION WITH MOSES AND ELIJAH AND GOD IN HEAVEN

B. MARK'S ACCOUNT OF THE TRANSFIGURATION WITH MOSES AND ELIJAH WITH JESUS CHRIST AND HIS HEAVENLY FATHER

The Apostle Mark also records the events of The Transfiguration when the Glory of God came upon Jesus Christ. Mark 9:1-8 proclaims and delivers this fact, "And he said unto them, Verily I say unto you, That there be some of them that stand here, which shall not taste of death, till they have seen the kingdom of God come with power. And after six days Jesus taketh with him Peter, and James, and John, and leadeth them up into an high mountain apart by themselves: and he was transfigured before them. And his raiment became shining, exceeding white as snow; so as no fuller on earth can white them. And there appeared unto them Elias with Moses: and they were talking with Jesus. And Peter answered and said to Jesus, Master, it is good for us to be here: and let us make three tabernacles; one for thee, and one for Moses, and one for Elias. For he wist not what to say; for they were sore afraid. And there was a cloud that overshadowed them: and a voice came out of the cloud, saying, This is my beloved Son: hear him. And suddenly, when they had looked round about, they saw no man any more, save Jesus only with themselves."(1041 KJV) This is also the second time that the Apostle John Mark testifies about hearing The Heavenly Father's Voice from Heaven speaking about His Son Jesus Christ. Jesus Christ is the Son of The Voice of the Clouds, Sun, and Sky. Jesus Christ is The Son of Creation. The Father of Jesus Christ is The Creator Himself.

THE TRINITY IS LIKE:
3 Triangles + 1 Triangle =
1 Big Triangle = 1 Big Folding Pyramid

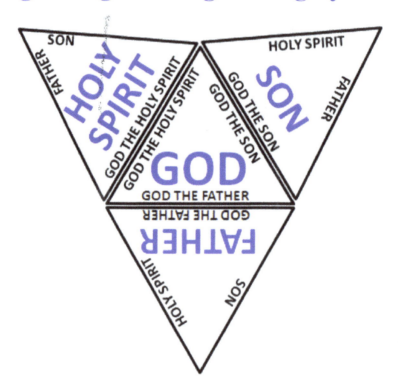

C. LUKE'S ACCOUNT OF THE TRANSFIGURATION WITH MOSES AND ELIJAH WITH JESUS CHRIST AND HIS HEAVENLY FATHER

The Apostle Luke records a second appearance of God The Heavenly Father saying that Jesus Christ is His Son. This time The Great Liberator Moses and The Prophet Elijah show up in the Transfiguration of Jesus Christ. God The Father audibly speaks out of the clouds of heaven and says that Jesus Christ is His Son. Luke 9:27-36 enlightens us and says, "See the kingdom of God. And it came to pass about eight days after these sayings, he took Peter and John and James, and went up into a mountain to pray. And as he prayed, the fashion of his countenance was altered, and his raiment was white as snow and glistering. And, behold, there talked with him two men, who were Moses and Elijah: Who appeared in glory, and spake of his decease which he should accomplish at Jerusalem. But Peter and they that were with him were heavy with sleep: and when they were awake, they saw his glory, and the two men that stood with him. And it came to pass, as they departed from him, Peter said unto Jesus, Master, it is good for us to be here: and let us make three tabernacles; one for thee, and one for Moses, and one for Elias: not knowing what he said. While he thus spake, there came a cloud, and over-shadowed them: and they feared as they entered into the cloud. And there came a voice out of the cloud, saying, 'This is my beloved Son: hear him'. And when the voice was past, Jesus was found alone. And they kept it close, and told no man in those days any of those things which they had seen."(KJV 1071) This is the second time that the Apostle Luke testifies about an audible voice from heaven of the Heavenly Father speaking about His Son Jesus Christ.

4

COMPARISON OF MATTHEW, MARK, LUKE, AND JOHN

A mathematical comparison of the Gospel of Matthew and the Gospel of Mark shows that over 90 percent of the Gospel of Mark is contained in the Gospel of Matthew. Another mathematical comparison shows clearly that over 50 percent of the Gospel of Mark is contained in the Gospel of Luke. Matthew and Luke both elaborated upon the writings of John Mark and this is one of the main reasons why both the Gospel of Matthew and the Gospel of Luke have more chapters than that of Mark. The Gospel of Mark has 16 Chapters. The Gospel of the Apostle Matthew who is also known as the Apostle Levi has 28 chapters. The Gospel of the Apostle Luke has 24 Chapters. The Gospel of Mark was very likely written in the years of approximately 50 A.D. The Gospels of Matthew and Luke are thought to have been written in the years of 60 A.D. or 70 A.D. The Apostle John Mark is thought to have been the key disciple and close associate of the Apostle Peter. The Apostle John Mark also went on a Missionary Journey with the Apostle Paul. The Apostle John Mark also went on a Missionary Journey with Barnabas to Cyprus. The Apostle John Mark was the scribe of the Apostle Peter that wrote down many of the preaching sermons of the Apostle Peter. The Gospel of Mark also may have some of the teachings and ideas of the Apostle Peter making the Gospel of Mark very connected to the preaching of the Apostle Peter. The Recipients of the Gospel of Mark are mostly those located in the city of Rome. The Main Theme of the Gospel of Mark is thought to be the essence of captivating Jesus Christ as the Son of God. The Synoptic Gospels are Three Gospels in 1 New Testament.

5

THE HOLY SPIRIT IS THE FATHER OF JESUS CHRIST

Luke writes about how the Holy Spirit is the Counselor and Teacher that teaches you what you ought to say because Luke 12:12 clearly states, "the Holy Spirit will teach you at that time what you should say."(KJV 1076) The Holy Spirit is also the Father of Jesus Christ in Luke 1:26-35, " In the sixth month of Elizabeth's pregnancy, God sent the angel Gabriel to Nazareth, a town in Galilee, to a virgin pledged to be married to a man named Joseph, a descendant of David. The virgin's name was Mary. The angel went to her and said, "Greetings, you who are highly favored! The Lord is with you." Mary was greatly troubled at his words and wondered what kind of greeting this might be. But the angel said to her, "Do not be afraid, Mary; you have found favor with God. You will conceive and give birth to a son, and you are to call him Jesus. He will be great and will be called the Son of the Most High. The Lord God will give him the throne of his father David, and he will reign over Jacob's descendants forever; his kingdom will never end." "How will this be," Mary asked the angel, "since I am a virgin?" The angel answered, "The Holy Spirit will come on you, and the power of the Most High will overshadow you. So the holy one to be born will be called the Son of God."(KJV 1056) The Trinity is fact because the Father in heaven is God Himself. One way that we see how the Father in Heaven is the Father of Jesus Christ in this passage is when the Father of Jesus Christ causes Mary to conceive. This happens as the angel Gabriel appears to Mary and informs her that she was going to have the Holy Spirit of God come upon her and she was going to get pregnant with the Son of God and tells her to call His Name Jesus. The Holy Angel Gabriel announces that Jesus Christ The Son of The Most High God would be born into Planet Earth to save all of sinful humanity from their sins. Simon Peter worshipped Jesus Christ as God in Luke 5:8-9 "When Simon Peter saw this, he fell at Jesus' knees and said, "Go away from me, Lord; I am a sinful man!" For he and all his companions were astonished at the catch of fish."(KJV 1056)

27

GOD IS IN CONTROL OF PLANET EARTH 100%

**LUKE'S VIEW OF JESUS CHRIST THE SHEPHERD OF
PLANET EARTH 100% WITH 99% SAVED SHEEP**

6

LUKE CHAPTER 15 THE CHURCH SHEEP OF JESUS CHRIST PLANET EARTH 100% WITH 99% SAVED SHEEP

If the number 100 in Luke Chapter 15 can be taken to be a percentage number like 100 Percent, then the parable of Luke 15 is about 99 percent salvation of the sheep. If this possibility can be true then Luke 15 is: The Parable of the 99 Percent Saved Sheep And One Percent Lost Sheep = 100%. Luke describes the parable of the one percent lost sheep and 99 percent saved sheep. The Apostle Luke gives us this new revelation of information and informs us in Luke 15:1-7 that says, "Then drew near unto him all the publicans and sinners for to hear him. And the Pharisees and scribes murmured, saying, This man receiveth sinners, and eateth with them. And he spake this parable unto them, saying, What man of you, having an hundred sheep, if he lose one of them, doth not leave the ninety and nine in the wilderness, and go after that which is lost, until he find it? And when he hath found it, he layeth it on his shoulders, rejoicing. And when he cometh home, he calleth together his friends and neighbours, saying unto them, Rejoice with me; for I have found my sheep which was lost. I say unto you, that likewise much rejoicing shall be done in heaven over one sinner that repenteth, more than over ninety and nine just persons, which need no repentance."(KJV 1081) The Church of Jesus Christ Planet Earth is 7.3 Billion People in Size if Jesus Christ is the Chief Shepherd of Planet Earth. Revelation 21:6 says, "It is done."(KJV 1356) It is very possible that these words are very likely to be true because Jesus Christ Himself actually spoke these words into reality in Luke Chapter 15. If Jesus Christ said 99 percent of the sheep on planet earth are saved would it even be possible? Some people think that in the near future all of planet Earth will belong to Jesus Christ 100 Percent. There are also some opinions that Jesus Christ has already taken over planet Earth 100 Percent and already finished the work 100%. If this is true then Jesus Christ is in 100 Percent full control of planet earth a is getting ready to remove all evil, demons, evil spirits, the Anti-Christ, and the Devil Himself completely off of planet Earth 100 Percent. Some people believe these ideas can be true and others have varying view points.

GOD IS THE CHIEF SHEPHERD OF PLANET EARTH 100 PERCENT

JESUS CHRIST IS THE SHEPHERD OF ALL SHEEP 100 PERCENT

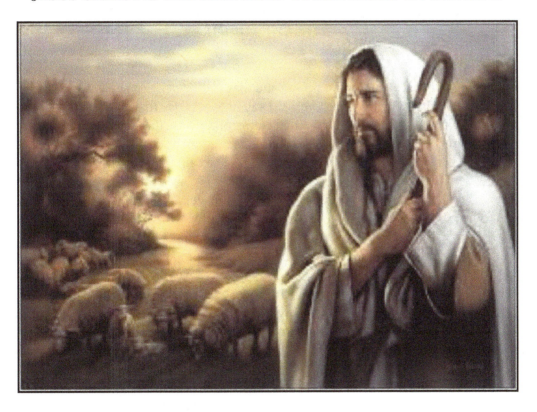

7

THE APOSTLE JOHN'S ACCOUNT OF JESUS CHRIST
THE SHEPHERD

Jesus Christ gives His sheep eternal life forever. One passage that tells from the Holy Bible that Jesus Christ is God and that the sheep belong to Jesus Christ is John 10:1-33 that states, "Verily, verily, I say unto you, He that entereth not by the door into the sheepfold, but climbeth up some other way, the same is a thief and a robber. But he that entereth in by the door is the shepherd of the sheep. To him the porter openeth; and the sheep hear his voice: and he calleth his own sheep by name, and leadeth them out. And when he putteth forth his own sheep, he goeth before them, and the sheep follow him: for they know his voice. And a stranger will they not follow, but will flee from him: for they know not the voice of strangers. This parable spake Jesus unto them: but they understood not what things they were which he spake unto them. Then said Jesus unto them again, Verily, verily, I say unto you, I am the door of the sheep. All that ever came before me are thieves and robbers: but the sheep did not hear them. I am the door: by me if any man enter in, he shall be saved, and shall go in and out, and find pasture. The thief cometh not, but for to steal, and to kill, and to destroy: I am come that they might have life, and that they might have it more abundantly. I am the good shepherd: the good shepherd giveth his life for the sheep. But he that is an hireling, and not the shepherd, whose own the sheep are not, seeth the wolf coming, and leaveth the sheep, and fleeth: and the wolf catcheth them, and scattereth the sheep. The hireling fleeth, because he is an hireling, and careth not for the sheep. I am the good shepherd, and know my sheep, and am known of mine. As the Father knoweth me, even so know I the Father: and I lay down my life for the sheep. And other sheep I have, which are not of this fold: them also I must bring, And they shall hear my voice; and there shall be one fold, and one shepherd. Therefore doth my Father love me, because I lay down my life, that I might take it again. No man taketh it from me, but I lay it down of myself. I have power to lay it down, and I have power to take it again. This commandment have I received of my Father. There was a division therefore again among the Jews for these sayings. And many of them said, He hath a devil, and is mad; why hear ye him? Others said, These are not the words of him that hath a devil. Can a devil open the eyes of the blind? And it was at Jerusalem the feast of the dedication, and it was winter. And Jesus walked in the temple in Solomon's porch. Then came the Jews round about him, and said unto him, How long dost thou make us to doubt? If thou be the Christ, tell us plainly. Jesus answered them, I told you, and ye believed not: the works that I do in my Father's name, they bear witness of me. But ye believe not, because ye are not of my sheep, as I said unto you. My sheep hear my voice, and I know them, and they follow me: And I give unto them eternal life; and they shall never perish, neither shall any man pluck them out of my hand. My Father, which gave them me, is greater than all; and no man is able to pluck them out of my Father's hand. I and my Father are one. Then the Jews took up stones again to stone him. Jesus answered them, Many good works have I shewed you from my Father; for which of those works do ye stone me? The Jews answered him, saying, For a good work we stone the not; but for blasphemy; and because that thou, being a man, makest thyself God."(KJV 1112) Here in this passage we see that Jesus Christ claims that He has the same essence of Deity that the Father has because Jesus says that they are one and have the same hand. The Church of Jesus Christ Planet Earth possibly has over 7.3 Billion Christians in it right now according to John 10 and Luke 15. If each sheep is worth 74 Million People Each then 99 Sheep X 74,000,000 = 7,300,000,000 sheep of Jesus Christ = 7.3 Billion Christians Now in accordance to this interpretation of Luke Chapter 15. Some people agree with this interpretation. Some people do not agree with this interpretation.

THE SHEPHERD OF ALL ETERNAL LIFE

8

THE FATHER IN HEAVEN GIVES YOU THE HOLY SPIRIT

Jesus speaks of the Holy Spirit and the Father also in John 14:26 that says, "But the Counselor, the Holy Spirit, whom the Father will send in my name, will teach you all things and will remind you of everything I have said to you."(KJV 1118) Another place where Jesus Christ mentions that the Father in Heaven would give the Holy Spirit to us in greater measure to testify of Him is in John 15:26 that proclaims, "When the Counselor comes, whom I will send to you from the Father, the Spirit of truth who goes out from the Father, he will testify about me."(KJV 1120) If we have the Holy Spirit we live in the Kingdom of God.

RAINING KEYS OF THE KINGDOM OF HEAVEN

9

THE KEYS OF THE KINGDOM OF GOD THE HEAVENLY FATHER

In the Book of Revelation Jesus Christ is King of Kings and LORD of LORD'S. Revelation 19:16 reveals, "And he hath on his vesture and on his thigh a name written, KING OF KINGS, AND LORD OF LORDS."(KJV 1288) When praying to God we are praying for His Kingdom to come on planet Earth. We become Kings and Lords as God so chooses to give us an opening into the Kingdom of Heaven. With the Keys of the Kingdom of Heaven we become Kings of the Kingdom of Heaven. The only place in the Holy Bible that the exact phrase "The Keys of The Kingdom of Heaven" is located is in Matthew 16:19 that passes on this information and knowledge on to you, "And I will give unto thee the keys of the kingdom of heaven: and whatsoever thou shalt bind on earth shall be bound in heaven: and whatsoever thou shalt loose on earth shall be loosed in heaven."(KJV 1011) Here in this Passage Jesus Christ gives you The Keys of the Kingdom of Heaven that are the Keys of The Kingdom of The Heavenly Father. The Gospel of Matthew is known as the Gospel of The Kingdom of Heaven.

JESUS CHRIST IS THE KING OF THE KINGDOM OF HEAVEN NOW

10

THE KINGDOM OF HEAVEN IS TAKEN BY THE FORCE OF THE FATHER IN HEAVEN

More and more Kingdom Boldness is in Matthew 11:12 that declares, "And from the days of John the Baptist until now the kingdom of heaven suffereth violence, and the violent take it by force."(KJV 1003) The things of the Kingdom are also in Matthew 6:31-34 that says, "Therefore take no thought, saying, What shall we eat? or, What shall we drink? or, Wherewithal shall we be clothed? (For after all these things do the Gentiles seek:) for your heavenly Father knoweth that ye have need of all these things. But seek ye first the kingdom of God, and his righteousness; and all these things shall be added unto you. Take therefore no thought for the morrow: for the morrow shall take thought for the things of itself. Sufficient unto the day is the evil thereof."(KJV 997) The Kingdom is a Mystery in The Holy Bible and the Apostles of Jesus Christ lived in the Kingdom of Heaven as also did the Prophets of God. The Kingdom of The Heavenly Father is simply this: Serving God with the Holy Spirit Gifts He has given you.

YOU NOW REAP THE HARVEST ON THE SEED THAT WAS SOWN

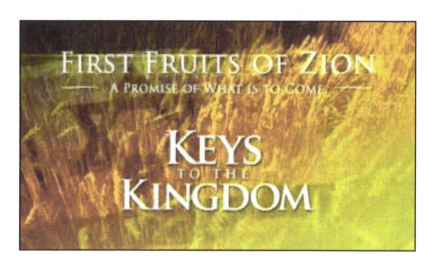

11

THE HEAVENLY KINGDOM OF THE HEAVENLY FATHER GIVES YOU 30,60, AND 100 TIMES WHAT YOU SOW IN HARVEST

The Apostle Mark also known as John Mark is the disciple that wrote the first gospel of Jesus Christ. If this is true John Mark was probably one of the best scribes in the days of the early apostles. This is certainly true when it comes to the Writings and Origins of the the Four Gospels. One of the main teachings of the Gospel of Mark is The Parable of the Sower that produces 30, 60, and 100 times more and as the stars of heaven for a multitude. Mark 4:1-20 declares, "Again Jesus began to teach by the lake. The crowd that gathered around him was so large that he got into a boat and sat in it out on the lake, while all the people were along the shore at the water's edge. He taught them many things by parables, and in his teaching said: "Listen! A farmer went out to sow his seed. As he was scattering the seed, some fell along the path, and the birds came and ate it up. Some fell on rocky places, where it did not have much soil. It sprang up quickly, because the soil was shallow. But when the sun came up, the plants were scorched, and they withered because they had no root. Other seed fell among thorns, which grew up and choked the plants, so that they did not bear grain. Still other seed fell on good soil. It came up, grew and produced a crop, some multiplying thirty, some sixty, some a hundred times. Then Jesus said, "Whoever has ears to hear, let them hear." When he was alone, the Twelve and the others around him asked him about the parables. He told them, "The secret of the kingdom of God has been given to you. But to those on the outside everything is said in parables so that, "'they may be ever seeing but never perceiving, and ever hearing but never understanding; otherwise they might *turn* and be forgiven!'" Then Jesus said to them, "Don't you understand this parable? How then will you understand any parable? The farmer sows the word. Some people are like seed along the path, where the word is sown. As soon as they hear it, Satan comes and takes away the word that was sown in them. Others, like seed sown on rocky places, hear the word and at once receive it with gladness. But since they have no root, they last only a short time. When trouble or persecution comes because of the word, they quickly fall away. Still others, like seed sown among thorns, hear the word; but the worries of this life, the deceitfulness of wealth and the desires for other things come in and choke the word, making it unfruitful. Others, like seed sown on good soil, hear the word, accept it, and produce a crop some thirty, some sixty, some a hundred times what was sown."(1034 KJV) People who sow seed in The Kingdom of God continually reap a harvest of 30, 60, 100, and 1000 times what they sowed and more!

THE FATHER IN HEAVEN HAS PUT ALL THINGS IN THE HANDS OF THE SON GOD AND HAS PUT ALL MATERIAL THINGS IN THE HANDS OF JESUS CHRIST. JESUS CHRIST WANTS TO GIVE US ALL MATERIAL THINGS SO MUCH THAT HE WENT TO THE CROSS OF CALVARY AND CAME BACK WITH OPEN HANDS. JESUS CHRIST HAS HIS OPEN HANDS READY TO GIVE YOU EVERYTHING YOU ASK OF HIM GENEROUSLY WITHOUT RESTRAINT OR HINDRANCE. JESUS CHRIST HAS AN ABUNDANT FLOWING RIVER OF BLESSINGS FLOWING FROM HIS OPEN HANDS INTO YOUR HANDS SO THAT YOU MAY RECEIVE HIS INCREASING MATERIAL BLESSINGS IN YOUR LIFE AND MINISTRY.

THE KEYS OF THE KINGDOM OF HEAVEN ARE GIVEN TO YOU NOW

THE SON IS THE KING OF ALL KINGS

12

THE HEAVENLY FATHER GIVES THE KINGDOM AND ALL THINGS TO THE SON

The Book of John also has many different amazing passages that describe the Heavenly Father to us. John 3:36+37 declares that God the Father has given all things into the hands of Jesus Christ when Jesus says, "The Father loveth the Son, and hath given all things into his hand. He that believeth on the Son hath everlasting life."(KJV 1100) Everything that the Father has, has been given over to the Son, because Jesus Christ is God Himself. A second scripture from the book of John that describes the relationship between the Heavenly Father and the Son Jesus Christ is John 5:22-23 that declares, "Moreover, the Father judges no one, but has entrusted all judgement to the Son, that all may honor the Son just as they honor the Father. He who does not honor the Son does not honor the Father who sent him."(KJV 1103) In this passage we see that all people must give the same honor that they give the Father to the Son also because Jesus Christ like the Heavenly Father is GOD Almighty.

The Jews were jealous of Jesus Christ because of the close relationship that He had with the Heavenly Father. This jealousy of the Jews is seen when they try to kill Him. John 10:33 says, "'We are not stoning you for any of these,' replied the Jews, 'but for blasphemy, because you a mere man, claim to be God.'"(NIV 2093) The reason the Jews said that Jesus Christ was claiming to be God was because He forgave sin and did other things that only GOD himself could do.

Another place where we see Jesus Christ speaking to his Heavenly Father was when he was going to get crucified in Mark 14:34-36 that says, "And saith unto them, My soul is exceeding sorrowful unto death: tarry ye here, and watch. And he went forward a little, and fell on the ground, and prayed that, if it were possible, the hour might pass from him. And he said, Abba, Father, all things are possible unto thee; take away this cup from me: nevertheless not what I will, but what thou wilt."(KJV 1051) Jesus Christ did not come to do his will when he was on Earth, but the will of the Father in Heaven. Jesus Christ would have probably preferred to be a King or some other personage of high stature. When Jesus Christ returns to planet He will be King of all Kings and LORD of all LORDS.

THE SON IS THE LORD OF ALL LORDS

13

MATTHEW AND THE KINGDOM OF CHRIST IS THE KINGDOM OF GOD IN MANIFESTATION NOW

The Gospel of Matthew is the most respected of the four Gospels when it comes to the Teaching of The Kingdom of Heaven and The Kingdom of God. The Kingdom of GOD is The Kingdom of Christ because the Main Character of The Holy Bible is Christ and He is the Word of God. The Holy Bible is the book of God about God. The Holy Bible is the book of Christ about Christ. The Gospel of Matthew talks about the coming of The Christ who is Jesus Christ the Messiah who has fulfilled over 300 different Old Testament Prophecies. Jesus Christ is the real Messiah and The Christ found in the famous phrase, "Keep The Christ in Christmas". If the Christ in Christmas refers to Jesus Christ it is very possible that every time a person says the famous phrase "Merry Christmas" that they are actually speaking out loud the Name of Jesus Christ in one way or another. The Kingdom of Heaven is found in the Book of Matthew over 30 times. Things are in Matthew 6:8-13 " Be not ye therefore like unto them: for your Father knoweth what things ye have need of, before ye ask him. After this manner therefore pray ye: Our Father which art in heaven, Hallowed be thy name. Thy kingdom come, Thy will be done in earth, as it is in heaven. Give us this day our daily bread. And forgive us our debts, as we forgive our debtors. And lead us not into temptation, but deliver us from evil: For thine is the kingdom, and the power, and the glory, for ever. Amen."(KJV 996) Kingdom Boldness is in Matthew 11:12 "And from the days of John the Baptist until now the kingdom of heaven suffereth violence, and the violent take it by force."(KJV 1003) The things of the Kingdom are also in Matthew 6:31-34 "Therefore take no thought, saying, What shall we eat? or, What shall we drink? or, Wherewithal shall we be clothed? (For after all these things do the Gentiles seek:) for your heavenly Father knoweth that ye have need of all these things. But seek ye first the kingdom of God, and his righteousness; and all these things shall be added unto you. Take therefore no thought for the morrow: for the morrow shall take thought for the things of itself. Sufficient unto the day is the evil thereof."(KJV 997) The Kingdom is a Mystery in The Holy Bible and the Apostles of Jesus Christ lived in the Kingdom of Heaven as also did the Prophets of God. The Kingdom of Heaven is simply this: Serving God with the Gifts He has given you in action to the best of your ability and capabilities. Ability is the skill and power needed to perform a specific task, job, and/or function. Capability is the affinity, potential, confidence, and experience applied when performing a specified ability or skill. This is done in an effective way producing continual positive results.

THE 12 APOSTLES OF JESUS CHRIST SENT TO PREACH HIS KINGDOM BECAUSE HE IS KING OF KINGS

GOD ✝ he SON

PART TWO:

God The Son In Jesus Christ

SON OF GOD

THE CHRIST CHILD IN TIME TRANSITION FROM B.C. TO A.D.

THE HOLY SPIRIT IS THE FATHER OF JESUS CHRIST

1

MATTHEW'S ACCOUNT OF THE BIRTH CHRIST OF JESUS

The First Two chapters of the book of Matthew speak of the Genealogy of Jesus Christ and the birth of Jesus Christ. The very first verse of the book of Matthew describes the relationship of Jesus Christ to King David. It is possible that King David earnestly prayed to God that his sons and descendants would produce the prophesied Messiah. In all actuality King David's physical son Solomon had one of the greatest Kingdoms in the History of planet earth. King David's Kingdom and King Solomon's Kingdom both lasted 40 years each. Jesus Christ is known as the Son of David. King David is known as the Son of Abraham in accordance to this scripture. Here in this passage it is very important to notice three main names that come in a very specific sequence. Abraham was Alive in the year 2000 B.C. King David was Alive in the year 1000 B.C. Jesus Christ was born in 7 B.C. and therefore Alive and 6 or 7 years of age in the Year Zero. The Year of Zero is the Transitional Year that Changed Actual History looking back through a Historical Glass from B.C.(Before Christ) to A.D.[Anno Domini or After Death(of Jesus Christ)]. Matthew 1:1-2:23 states, "The book of the generation of Jesus Christ, the son of David, the son of Abraham. Abraham begat Isaac; and Isaac begat Jacob; and Jacob begat Judas and his brethren; And Judas begat Phares and Zara of Thamar; and Phares begat Esrom; and Esrom begat Aram; And Aram begat Aminadab; and Aminadab begat Naasson; and Naasson begat Salmon; And Salmon begat Booz of Rachab; and Booz begat Obed of Ruth; and Obed begat Jesse; And Jesse begat David the king; and David the king begat Solomon of her that had been the wife of Urias; And Solomon begat Roboam; and Roboam begat Abia; and Abia begat Asa; And Asa begat Josaphat; and Josaphat begat Joram; and Joram begat Ozias; And Ozias begat Joatham; and Joatham begat Achaz; and Achaz begat Ezekias; And Ezekias begat Manasses; and Manasses begat Amon; and Amon begat Josias; And Josias begat Jechonias and his brethren, about the time they were carried away to Babylon: And after they were brought to Babylon, Jechonias begat Salathiel; and Salathiel begat Zorobabel; And Zorobabel begat

Abiud; and Abiud begat Eliakim; and Eliakim begat Azor; And Azor begat Sadoc; and Sadoc begat Achim; and Achim begat Eliud; And Eliud begat Eleazar; and Eleazar begat Matthan; and Matthan begat Jacob; And Jacob begat Joseph the husband of Mary, of whom was born Jesus, who is called Christ. So all the generations from Abraham to David are fourteen generations; and from David until the carrying away into Babylon are fourteen generations; and from the carrying away into Babylon unto Christ are fourteen generations. Now the birth of Jesus Christ was on this wise: When as his mother Mary was espoused to Joseph, before they came together, she was found with child of the Holy Ghost. Then Joseph her husband, being a just man, and not willing to make her a public example, was minded to put her away privily. But while he thought on these things, behold, the angel of the LORD appeared unto him in a dream, saying, Joseph, thou son of David, fear not to take unto thee Mary thy wife: for that which is conceived in her is of the Holy Ghost. And she shall bring forth a son, and thou shalt call his name JESUS: for he shall save his people from their sins. Now all this was done, that it might be fulfilled which was spoken of the Lord by the prophet, saying, Behold, a virgin shall be with child, and shall bring forth a son, and they shall call his name Emmanuel, which being interpreted is, God with us. Then Joseph being raised from sleep did as the angel of the Lord had bidden him, and took unto him his wife: And knew her not till she had brought forth her firstborn son: and he called his name JESUS. Now when Jesus was born in Bethlehem of Judaea in the days of Herod the king, behold, there came wise men from the east to Jerusalem, Saying, Where is he that is born King of the Jews? for we have seen his star in the east, and are come to worship him. When Herod the king had heard these things, he was troubled, and all Jerusalem with him. And when he had gathered all the chief priests and scribes of the people together, he demanded of them where Christ should be born. And they said unto him, In Bethlehem of Judaea: for thus it is written by the prophet, And thou Bethlehem, in the land of Juda, art not the least among the princes of Juda: for out of thee shall come a Governor, that shall rule my people Israel. Then Herod, when he had privily called the wise men, enquired of them diligently what time the star appeared. And he sent them to Bethlehem, and said, Go and search diligently for the young child; and when ye have found him, bring me word again, that I may come and worship him also. When they had heard the king, they departed; and, lo, the star, which they saw in the east, went before them, till it came and stood over where the young child was. When they saw the star, they rejoiced with exceeding great happiness. And when they were come into the house, they saw the young child with Mary his mother, and fell down, and worshipped him: and when they had opened their treasures, they presented unto him gifts; gold, and frankincense and myrrh. And being warned of God in a dream that they should not return to Herod, they departed into their own country another way. And when they were departed, behold, the angel of the Lord appeareth to Joseph in a dream, saying,

Arise, and take the young child and his mother, and flee into Egypt, and be thou there until I bring thee word: for Herod will seek the young child to destroy him. When he arose, he took the young child and his mother by night, and departed into Egypt: And was there until the death of Herod: that it might be fulfilled which was spoken of the Lord by the prophet, saying, Out of Egypt have I called my son. Then Herod, when he saw that he was mocked of the wise men, was exceeding wroth, and sent forth, and slew all the children that were in Bethlehem, and in all the coasts thereof, from two years old and under, according to the time which he had diligently inquired of the wise men. Then was fulfilled that which was spoken by Jeremiah the prophet, saying, In Rama was there a voice heard, lamentation, and weeping, and great mourning, Rachel weeping for her children, and would not be comforted, because they are not. But when Herod was dead, behold, an angel of the Lord appeareth in a dream to Joseph in Egypt, Saying, Arise, and take the young child and his mother, and go into the land of Israel: for they are dead which sought the young child's life. And he arose, and took the young child and his mother, and came into the land of Israel. But when he heard that Archelaus did reign in Judaea in the room of his father Herod, he was afraid to go thither: notwithstanding, being warned of God in a dream, he turned aside into the parts of Galilee: And he came and dwelt in a city called Nazareth: that it might be fulfilled which was spoken by the prophets, He shall be called a Nazarene."(KJV 1037) There are many Generations from Adam the First Created man to Jesus Christ the Number One Created Man of all Number One men.

THE CHRIST IN CHRISTMAS IS THE SAVIOR OF ALL SOULS

2

THREE SETS OF 14 GENERATION EQUALS 42 GENERATIONS FROM ABRAHAM TO JESUS CHRIST

The Book of Matthew records that there are 14 generations from Abraham to King David. This time period is a time of 1000 years from 2000 B.C. to 1000B.C. There are also 14 generations from King David to the Exile of Babylon in 597 B.C. The next 14 generations occur from The Exile of Babylon in 597 B.C. to the Birth of Jesus Christ in 7 B.C.. Fourteen generations plus fourteen generations plus fourteen generation is Forty Two Generations from Father Abraham to Our LORD AND SAVIOR JESUS CHRIST. This total time period from Abraham to Christ was exactly 2000 years.

14 Generations From Abraham to King David (1000 Years)
14 Generations From King David to the Exile of Babylon(Jeremiah)(400 Years)
14 Generations From Exile of Babylon to The Birth of Jesus Christ(600 Years)
42 Generations From Abraham to Jesus Christ (2000 Years)

A Generation of Generations
A Generation is 40 x 40 = 1600
42 Generations x 48 = 2016

THE ANGEL OF THE LORD BECOMES THE CHRIST CHILD

3

LUKE'S ACCOUNT OF THE BIRTH OF JESUS CHRIST

The first two chapters of the book of Luke are very similar to the first two chapters of the book of Matthew. The Apostle Matthew in his first two chapters talks about the birth of Jesus Christ. The Apostle Luke in the first two chapters of his book also records the events of The Birth of Jesus Christ the Savior of the World. Luke 1 + 2 declares, "Forasmuch as many have taken in hand to set forth in order a declaration of those things which are most surely believed among us, Even as they delivered them unto us, which from the beginning were eyewitnesses, and ministers of the word; It seemed good to me also, having had perfect understanding of all things from the very first, to write unto thee in order, most excellent Theophilus, That thou mightest know the certainty of those things, wherein thou hast been instructed. There was in the days of Herod, the king of Judaea, a certain priest named Zacharias, of the course of Abia: and his wife was of the daughters of Aaron, and her name was Elisabeth. And they were both righteous before God, walking in all the commandments and ordinances of the Lord blameless. And they had no child, because that Elisabeth was barren, and they both were now well stricken in years. And it came to pass, that while he executed the priest's office before God in the order of his course, According to the custom of the priest's office, his lot was to burn incense when he went into the temple of the Lord. And the whole multitude of the people were praying without at the time of incense. And there appeared unto him an angel of the Lord standing on the right side of the altar of incense. And when Zacharias saw him, he was troubled, and fear fell upon him. But the angel said unto him, Fear not, Zacharias: for thy prayer is heard; and thy wife Elisabeth shall bear thee a son, and thou shalt call his name John. And thou shalt have happiness and gladness; and many shall rejoice at his birth. For he shall be great in the sight of the Lord, and shall drink neither wine nor strong drink; and he shall be filled with the Holy Ghost, even from his mother's womb. And many of the children of Israel shall he turn to the Lord their God. And he shall go before him in the spirit and power of Elias, to turn the hearts of the fathers to the children, and the disobedient to the wisdom of the just; to make ready a people prepared for the Lord. And Zacharias said unto the angel, Whereby shall I know this? for I am an old man, and my wife well stricken in years. And the angel answering said unto him, I am Gabriel, that stand in the presence of God; and am sent to speak unto thee, and to shew thee these glad tidings. And, behold, thou shalt be dumb, and not able to speak, until the day that these things shall be performed, because thou believest not my words, which shall be fulfilled in their season. And the people waited for Zacharias, and marvelled that he tarried so long in the temple. And when he came out, he could not speak unto them: and they perceived that he had seen a vision in the temple: for he beckoned unto them, and remained speechless. And it came to pass, that, as soon as the days of his ministration were accomplished, he departed to his own house. And after those days his wife Elisabeth conceived, and hid herself five months, saying, Thus hath the Lord dealt with me in the days wherein he looked on me, to take away my reproach among men. And in the sixth month the angel Gabriel was sent from God unto a city of Galilee, named Nazareth, To a virgin espoused to a man whose name was Joseph, of the house of David; and the virgin's name was Mary. And the angel came in unto her, and said, Hail, thou that art highly favoured, the Lord is with thee: blessed art thou among women. And when she saw him, she was troubled at his saying, and cast in her mind what manner of salutation this should be. And the angel said unto her, Fear not, Mary: for thou hast found favour with God. And, behold, thou shalt conceive in thy womb, and bring forth a son, and shalt call his name JESUS. He shall be great, and shall be called the Son of the Highest: and the Lord God shall give unto him the throne of his father David: And he shall reign over the house of Jacob for ever; and of his kingdom there shall be no end. Then said Mary unto the angel, How shall this be, seeing I know not a man? And the angel answered and said unto her, The Holy Ghost shall come upon thee, and the power of the Highest shall overshadow thee: therefore also that holy thing which shall be born of thee shall be called the Son of God. And, behold, thy cousin Elisabeth, she hath also conceived a son in her old age: and this is the sixth month with her, who was called barren. For with God nothing shall be impossible. And Mary said, Behold the handmaid of the Lord; be it unto me according to thy word. And the angel departed from her. And Mary arose in those days, and went into the hill country with haste, into a city of Juda; And entered into the house of Zacharias, and saluted Elisabeth. And it came to pass, that, when Elisabeth heard the salutation of Mary, the babe leaped in her womb; and Elisabeth was filled with the Holy Ghost: And she spake out with a loud voice, and said, Blessed art thou among women, and blessed is the fruit of thy womb. And whence is this to me, that the mother of my Lord should come to me? For, lo, as soon as the voice of thy salutation sounded in mine ears, the babe leaped in my womb for happiness. And blessed is she that believed: for there shall be a performance of those things which were told her from the Lord. And Mary said, My soul doth magnify the Lord, And my spirit hath rejoiced in God my Saviour. For he hath regarded the low estate of his handmaiden: for, behold, from henceforth all generations shall call me blessed. For he that is mighty hath done to me great things; and holy is his name. And his mercy is on them that fear him from generation to generation. He hath shewed strength with his arm; he hath scattered the proud in the imagination of their hearts. He hath put down the mighty from their seats, and exalted them of low a degree. He hath filled the hungry with good things; and the rich he hath sent empty away. He hath helped his servant Israel, in remembrance of his mercy; As he spake to our fathers, to Abraham, and to his seed for ever. And Mary abode with her about three months, and returned to her own house. Now Elisabeth's full time came that she should be delivered; and she brought forth a son. And her neighbours and her cousins heard how the Lord had shewed great mercy upon her; and they rejoiced with her. And it came to pass, that on the eighth day they came to circumcise the child; and they called him Zacharias, after the name of his father. And his mother answered and said, Not so; but he shall be called John. And they said unto her, There is none of thy kindred that is called by this name. And they made signs to his father, how he would have him called. And he asked for a writing table, and wrote, saying, His name is John. And they marvelled all. And his mouth was opened immediately, and his tongue loosed, and he spake, and praised God. And fear came on all that dwelt round about them: and all these sayings were noised abroad throughout all the hill country of Judaea. And all they that heard them laid them up in their hearts, saying, What manner of child shall this be! And the hand of the Lord was with him. And his father Zacharias was filled with the Holy Ghost, and prophesied, saying, Blessed be the Lord God of Israel; for he hath visited and redeemed his people, And hath raised up an horn of salvation for us in the house of his servant David; As he spake by the mouth of his holy prophets, which have been since the world began: That we should be saved from our enemies, and from the hand of all that hate us; To perform the mercy promised to our fathers, and to remember his holy covenant; The oath which he sware to our father Abraham, That he would grant unto us, that we being delivered out of the hand of our enemies might serve him without fear, In holiness and righteousness before him, all the days of our life. And thou, child, shalt be called the prophet of the Highest: for thou shalt go before the face of the Lord to prepare his ways; To give knowledge of salvation unto his people by the remission of their sins, Through the tender mercy of our God; whereby the dayspring from on high hath visited us, To give light to them that sit in darkness and in the shadow of death, to guide our feet into the way of peace. And the child grew, and waxed strong in spirit, and was in the deserts till the day of his shewing unto Israel. And it came to pass in those days, that there went out a decree from Caesar Augustus that all the world should be taxed. (And this taxing was first made when Cyrenius was governor of Syria.)

And all went to be taxed, every one into his own city. And Joseph also went up from Galilee, out of the city of Nazareth, into Judaea, unto the city of David, which is called Bethlehem; (because he was of the house and lineage of David:) To be taxed with Mary his espoused wife, being great with child. And so it was, that, while they were there, the days were accomplished that she should be delivered. And she brought forth her firstborn son, and wrapped him in swaddling clothes, and laid him in a manger; because there was no room for them in the inn. And there were in the same country shepherds abiding in the field, keeping watch over their flock by night. And, lo, the angel of the Lord came upon them, and the glory of the Lord shone round about them: and they were sore afraid. And the angel said unto them, Fear not: for, behold, I bring you good tidings of great joy, which shall be to all people. For unto you is born this day in the city of David a Saviour, which is Christ the Lord. And this shall be a sign unto you; Ye shall find the babe wrapped in swaddling clothes, lying in a manger. And suddenly there was with the angel a multitude of the heavenly host praising God, and saying, Glory to God in the highest, and on earth peace, good will toward men. And it came to pass, as the angels were gone away from them into heaven, the shepherds said one to another, Let us now go even unto Bethlehem, and see this thing which is come to pass, which the Lord hath made known unto us. And they came with haste, and found Mary, and Joseph, and the babe lying in a manger. And when they had seen it, they made known abroad the saying which was told them concerning this child. And all they that heard it wondered at those things which were told them by the shepherds. But Mary kept all these things, and pondered them in her heart. And the shepherds returned, glorifying and praising God for all the things that they had heard and seen, as it was told unto them. And when eight days were accomplished for the circumcising of the child, his name was called JESUS, which was so named of the angel before he was conceived in the womb. And when the days of her purification according to the law of Moses were accomplished, they brought him to Jerusalem, to present him to the Lord; (As it is written in the law of the LORD, Every male that openeth the womb shall be called holy to the Lord;) And to offer a sacrifice according to that which is said in the law of the Lord, A pair of turtledoves, or two young pigeons. And, behold, there was a man in Jerusalem, whose name was Simeon; and the same man was just and devout, waiting for the consolation of Israel: and the Holy Ghost was upon him. And it was revealed unto him by the Holy Ghost, that he should not see death, before he had seen the Lord's Christ. And he came by the Spirit into the temple: and when the parents brought in the child Jesus, to do for him after the custom of the law, Then took he him up in his arms, and blessed God, and said, Lord, now lettest thou thy servant depart in peace, according to thy word: For mine eyes have seen thy salvation, Which thou hast prepared before the face of all people; A light to lighten the Gentiles, and the glory of thy people Israel. And Joseph and his mother marvelled at those things which were spoken of him. And Simeon blessed them, and said unto Mary his mother, Behold, this child is set for the fall and rising again of many in Israel; and for a sign which shall be spoken against; (Yea, a sword shall pierce through thy own soul also,) that the thoughts of many hearts may be revealed. And there was one Anna, a prophetess, the daughter of Phanuel, of the tribe of Aser: she was of a great age, and had lived with an husband seven years from her virginity; And she was a widow of about fourscore and four years, which departed not from the temple, but served God with fastings and prayers night and day. And she coming in that instant gave thanks likewise unto the Lord, and spake of him to all them that looked for redemption in Jerusalem. And when they had performed all things according to the law of the Lord, they returned into Galilee, to their own city Nazareth. And the child grew, and waxed strong in spirit, filled with wisdom: and the grace of God was upon him. Now his parents went to Jerusalem every year at the feast of the passover. And when he was twelve years old, they went up to Jerusalem after the custom of the feast. And when they had fulfilled the days, as they returned, the child Jesus tarried behind in Jerusalem; and Joseph and his mother knew not of it. But they, supposing him to have been in the company, went a day's journey; and they sought him among their kinsfolk and acquaintance. And when they found him not, they turned back again to Jerusalem, seeking him. And it came to pass, that after three days they found him in the temple, sitting in the midst of the doctors, both hearing them, and asking them questions. And all that heard him were astonished at his understanding and answers. And when they saw him, they were amazed: and his mother said unto him, Son, why hast thou thus dealt with us? behold, thy father and I have sought thee sorrowing. And he said unto them, How is it that ye sought me? wist ye not that I must be about my Father's business? And they understood not the saying which he spake unto them. And he went down with them, and came to Nazareth, and was subject unto them: but his mother kept all these sayings in her heart. And Jesus increased in wisdom and stature, and in favour with God and man."(KJV 1057)

JESUS CHRIST IS SAVIOR AT HIS BIRTH

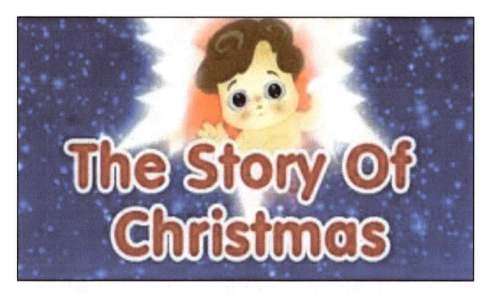

THE MAIN STORY OF CHRISTMAS IS JESUS CHRIST
THE MAIN STORY OF THE HOLY BIBLE IS JESUS CHRIST
THE HOLY BIBLE AND CHRISTMAS ARE BOTH ABOUT JESUS CHRIST
THE STORY OF CHRISTMAS IS THE STORY OF JESUS CHRIST
THE SAVIOR
THE STORY OF THE HOLY BIBLE IS THE STORY OF CHRIST
THE SAVIOR

4

HOLIDAYS ARE CONNECTED TO GOD AND JESUS CHRIST

All the Main Holidays of the Year are somehow connected to Jesus Christ and Religious Services because they are Holy Days of God. The Holidays of the year are like pieces of a puzzle of God Days that come together into one big puzzle picture. The Christmas Holiday is about Jesus Christ The Savior being born to Earth. Easter is the Holiday about the main part of Jesus Christ and that is Him giving His Perfect life at The Cross of Calvary. The Christ Tree of Christmas is The Same Christ Tree of Easter and Good Friday. St. Patrick's Day is about the Evangelist St. Patrick that was the first person to bring the Good News of Jesus Christ to all of Ireland. The Thanksgiving Holiday is about giving thanks to this same God for all of His Great Prosperity, Blessings, and Provisions. Holloween is about Ghosts and Spirits and Candy for Kids. Valentine's Day is about Love. The Holy Bible says that God is Love. Happy Holidays is equal to Happy Holy Days. Jesus Christ died on the Tree with green leaves of the Cross of Calvary in order to erase 100 percent of all our sins past, present, and future. We gain independence from the oppression of the Devil and 100 Percent of All Demons in The Blood of Jesus Christ.

THE PRE-INCARNATE CHRIST IS THE ANGEL OF THE LORD

5

JESUS CHRIST IS BORN THE SAVIOR OF THE WORLD

The Birth of Jesus Christ is Celebrated on the 25th of December of each year. Jesus Christ was not born on December 25, in the year 7 B.C. in accordance to some recorded history accounts. Jesus Christ was born around the year 6 or 7 B.C. Jesus Christ is born the Savior of the world. Isaiah 9:6+7 says, "For unto us a child is born, unto us a son is given: and the government shall be upon his shoulder: and his name shall be called Wonderful, Counsellor, The mighty God, The everlasting Father, The Prince of Peace. Of the increase of his government and peace there shall be no end, upon the throne of David, and upon his kingdom, to order it, and to establish it with judgment and with justice from henceforth even for ever. The zeal of the Lord of hosts will perform this. The Lord sent a word into Jacob, and it hath lighted upon Israel. And all the people shall know, even Ephraim and the inhabitant of Samaria."(KJV 733)

Some of the Names and Titles of Jesus Christ found in Isaiah Chapter 9 include: Mighty God, Everlasting, Father, Prince of Peace, Peace, Counselor, Wonderful, Sell, Light, King, Kingdom Throne of David = Son of David, Increase, Government, Judgment, Justice, Perform, God of Israel, Mighty, God, Establish, Throne, LORD, Order, Everlasting God, LORD of Hosts, God of Jacob, God of Israel, and Light of Israel.

JESUS CHRIST THE SAVIOR OF THE WORLD

6

THREE MEN VISIT ABRAHAM IN GENESIS CHAPTER 18

THE TRINITY VISITS ABRAHAM

Three Amazing Mysterious Visitors pay a visit to Abraham and cause Abraham to take heed and pay very close attention and be very attentive in attending to them. The LORD GOD is Three Persons in One God. Genesis 18:1-15 reveals three visitors from heaven, "The LORD appeared to Abraham near the great **tree**s of Mamre while he was sitting at the entrance to his tent in the heat of the day. Abraham looked up and saw three men standing nearby. When he saw them, he hurried from the entrance of his tent to meet them and bowed low to the ground.

He said, "If I have found favor in your eyes, my lord, do not pass your servant by. Let a little water be brought, and then you may all wash your feet and rest under this **tree**. Let me get you something to eat, so you can be refreshed and then go on your way now that you have come to your servant." "Very well," they answered, "do as you say." So Abraham hurried into the tent to Sarah. "Quick," he said, "get three seahs of the finest flour and knead it and bake some bread." Then he ran to the herd and selected a choice, tender calf and gave it to a servant, who hurried to prepare it. He then brought some curds and milk and the calf that had been prepared, and set these before them. While they ate, he stood near them under a **tree**. "Where is your wife Sarah?" they asked him. "There, in the tent," he said. Then one of them said, "I will surely return to you about this time next year, and Sarah your wife will have a son." Now Sarah was listening at the entrance to the tent, which was behind him. Abraham and Sarah were already very old, and Sarah was past the age of childbearing. So Sarah laughed to herself as she thought, "After I am worn out and my lord is old, will I now have this pleasure?" Then the LORD said to Abraham, "Why did Sarah laugh and say, 'Will I really have a child, now that I am old?' Is anything too hard for the LORD? I will return to you at the appointed time next year, and Sarah will have a son." Sarah was afraid, so she lied and said, "I did not laugh." But he said, "Yes, you did laugh."(NIV 39) It is interesting to note that at the beginning of the passage the Word Tree is seen multiple times. The Word tree appears in this passage three different times. Three Persons in three separate bodies visited Abraham. At the Crucifixion of Jesus Christ there were three separate trees with three different bodies, one on each tree.

This same GOD of Genesis 18 is the same LORD that confirmed the Word He had Already Given Abraham in Genesis Chapter 17. The LORD GOD tells Abraham that he will have a son when He changes the name of Sarai to Sarah. Genesis 17:15-27 declares, "God also said to Abraham, "As for Sarai your wife, you are no longer to call her Sarai; her name will be Sarah. I will bless her and will surely give you a son by her. I will bless her so that she will be the mother of nations; kings of peoples will come from her." Abraham fell facedown; he laughed and said to himself, "Will a son be born to a man a hundred years old? Will Sarah bear a child at the age of ninety?" And Abraham said to God, "If only Ishmael might live under your blessing!" Then God said, "Yes, but your wife Sarah will bear you a son, and you will call him Isaac. I will establish my covenant with him as an everlasting covenant for his descendants after him. And as for Ishmael, I have heard you: I will surely bless him; I will make him fruitful and will greatly increase his numbers. He will be the father of twelve rulers, and I will make him into a great nation. But my covenant I will establish with Isaac, whom Sarah will bear to you by this time next year." When he had finished speaking with Abraham, God went up from him. On that very day Abraham took his son Ishmael and all those born in his household or bought with his money, every male in his household, and circumcised them, as God told him. Abraham was ninety-nine years old when he was circumcised, and his son Ishmael was thirteen; Abraham and his son Ishmael were both circumcised on that very day. And every male in Abraham's household, including those born in his household or bought from a foreigner, was circumcised with him."(NIV 39) If Ishmael is a great nation then Ishmael and the vast majority of his descendants are very possibly saved in Jesus Christ.

THE CHRIST TREE = THE CHRISTMAS TREE

THE CHRIST TREE = THE CROSS OF CALVARY

7

THE TRADITION OF THE CHRIST TREE AT CHRISTMAS TIME IS TRUE BECAUSE THE CHRIST TREE IS THE CHRISTMAS TREE

The tradition of the Christ Tree at Christmas time deals with the most famous tree during Christmas Time. The most famous Tree at Christmas time is The Christmas Tree. To some people The Christmas Tree symbolizes the coming together of family. To other people the Christmas Tree symbolizes the giving and exchange of Christmas Gifts. Some people see the Christmas Tree and decorations as a method of making more money and selling more goods. The Christmas Tree and decorations to some people are a form of neighborly competition for home decorations. So it is clear to see that at Christmas Time The Christmas Tree serves as many different functions to many different people. Some people even gather around The Christmas Tree and sing songs that may include songs of Praise to God. The Christmas Tree is also about Jesus Christ giving His Life on The Cross of Calvary to forgive all the sins of all humanity 100% and all sins on Planet Earth 100 Percent. Jesus Christ is The Reason for The Season.

What is the reason for the season exactly? The Reason for The Season is Jesus Christ. What does that mean? What did Jesus Christ do? Jesus Christ has given us the answer to eternal life. The Reason may also be connected to the Reason in the following question: Do you know the Main Reason that you are going to have eternal life in heaven forever? The Reason in this Question is the very Same Reason of the Season of Christmas Time. The Reason for The Season is Jesus Christ dying on The Cross of Calvary to forgive all the sins of all humanity and remove all sin from planet Earth 100 Percent. The Prophet Isaiah tells us to come together and Reason together. The Reason Jesus Christ died on the Cross of Calvary and The Reason for the Season is one and the same. Isaiah 1:18+19 declares, "Come now, and let us reason together, saith the LORD: though your sins be as scarlet, they shall be as white as snow; though they be red like crimson, they shall be as wool. If ye be willing and obedient, ye shall eat the good of the land"(KJV 761) Christ is The Savior of The World. Keeping The Christ in

Christmas is Keeping The Power of Eternal Life in The Holiday Season of each and every Christmas every single year.

The Nativity Scene is also displayed at Christmas time with Shepherds and animals. Jesus Christ is shown as the child born in the Nativity celebrated on Christmas morning right next to the Christmas Tree. The Nativity scene is the depiction of the events of The Christ Child being born in a manger.

Martin Luther is Said to have found the Tradition of the Christmas Tree. Martin Luther as a young man liked to look at all the stars in the sky. So one day Martin Luther in order to simulate a scene of the stars in the sky put candles in a tree. This idea took off and many people wanted to have their very own tree with candles in it because the scene was spectacular to the eyes of the beholder. Matthew 6:22 shows, "The Eye is the lamp of the body."(KJV 1043) Jesus Christ was held to a tree by three nails: One in His Right Hand, One in His Left Hand, & One in His Feet. The Christ Tree, or better known as "The Christmas Tree", comes in many different varieties including the evergreen tree, the spruce, the pine, or the fir. This tree is connected to the celebration of the Christmas Holiday that is founded in the Christmas Story of Jesus Christ. Other types of trees that are not naturally grown trees are artificial trees. These Trees resemble a Green Christmas Tree and are made from polyvinyl chloride(PVC). The candles on a tree eventually became electronic lights. The Ornaments on the Christmas Tree vary in many colors and shapes. Some of the items that are placed at the top of the Christmas tree are Stars and The Holy Angels that sang rejoicing at the birth of Jesus Christ Our LORD and Savior.

MERRY CHRISTMAS IS EVANGELISM ABOUT THE CHRIST TREE

The Tradition of the Christmas Tree comes from the country of Germany. The actual tradition of the Green Christmas Tree is thought to have first started in the 15th Century or possibly in the 16th Century. The most religious and devoted Christians brought the actual Christmas Tree inside their houses to Celebrate the Birth of Jesus Christ the Savior of the world. Luke 2:11 "For unto you is born this day in the city of David a Savior, that is Christ the Lord." Many people saw how other people had a Christmas Tree inside their house and they wanted to have one inside their own home also. The Christmas Tree became more and more popular in more and more homes and eventually spread beyond Germany into other countries in the 17th and 18th centuries.

A Better understanding of the Cross of Calvary is achieved by knowing the original Greek word for the Tree that Jesus Christ was Crucified On. This is the Cross. The Strong's Concordance defines a tree as a piece of wood: #3586 xulon(xoo lon) is defined as timber as for fuel or material; a stick, club, or tree, or other wooden article or substance: a staff, a tree.(Strong's Greek 50)

Vine's Dictionary defines a tree as anything that is made of wood. Xulon 3586 (A) wood, a piece of wood, anything made of wood. Is used as a rendering "tree" in Luke 23:31, where the "Green Tree" refers either to Christ figuratively of all his Living Power and Excellencies, (B) "The Cross" the tree being the stauros , the upright pale(pole) or stake used by Romans in the Roman Army.(Vines 683)

8

THE TRADITION OF THE CHRIST TREE AT CHURCH DURING CHRISTMAS IS THE CROSS OF CALVARY

At Church the Christ Tree is seen as a Cross made of wood or some other material. The Cross is displayed in a prominent place outside churches and inside churches. Some churches have a Cross with no body of Jesus Christ on it because Jesus Christ has been Resurrected and He is Risen. Other Churches have a Cross with a body of Jesus Christ on it with a Crown of Thorns. This type of Cross is called a Crucifix depicting the Crucifixion of Jesus Christ with a Crown of Thorns dying for our sins by giving His perfect blood on the Cross of Calvary. It is the same Cross made from the same wood Tree. The most famous tree of all time is the tree that was used to make The Cross of Calvary. That Wood was the best wood used for the best work of the salvation of all of humanity that would choose to celebrate the Christ in Christmas and be saved forever in heaven. Christmas is about eternal salvation.

In the Second Chapter of First Peter it is clearly stated in the King James Version of the Holy Bible that The Cross of Calvary Is "The Tree". The New International Version Translation of the very same passage says that The Cross of Calvary is "The Cross". 1 Peter 2:24 "Who his own self bare our sins in his own body on the tree, that we, being dead to sins, should live unto righteousness: by whose stripes ye were healed."(KJV 1322) 1 Peter 2:24 "He himself bore our sins in his body on the cross, so that we might die to sins and live for righteousness; by his wounds you have been healed."(NIV 2448)

In the Fifth Chapter of The Book of Acts it is clearly stated in the King James Version of the Holy Bible that The Cross of Calvary Is "A Tree". The New International Version Translation of the very same passage says that The Cross of Calvary is "A Cross". Acts 5:30 "The God of our fathers raised up Jesus, whom ye slew and hanged on a tree."(KJV 1186) Acts 5:30 "God... raised Jesus from the dead whom you killed by hanging him on a cross."(NIV 2145)

In the Tenth Chapter of The Book of Acts it is clearly stated in the King James Version of the Holy Bible that The Cross of Calvary Is "A Tree". The New International Version Translation of the very same passage says that The Cross of Calvary is "A Cross". Acts 10:39 "They slew and hanged on a tree."(KJV 1195)

Acts 10:39 "They killed him by hanging him on a cross."(NIV 2162)

THE CHRIST TREE IS THE CROSS OF CALVARY

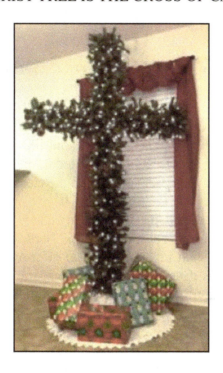

9

JESUS CHRIST ON THE CROSS OF CALVARY REMOVED
ALL SIN 100%

Jesus Christ On The Cross Of Calvary Removed All Sins And Curses 100% Forever! Psalm 22:14-16 says, "I am poured out like water, and all my bones are out of joint: my heart is like wax; it is melted in the midst of my bowels. My strength is dried up like a potsherd; and my tongue cleaveth to my jaws; and thou hast brought me into the dust of death. For dogs have compassed me: the assembly of the wicked have inclosed me: they pierced my hands and my feet."(NIV 1040)

Isaiah 53:10-12 declares, "Yet it pleased the Lord to bruise him; he hath put him to grief: when thou shalt make his soul an offering for sin, he shall see his seed, he shall prolong his days, and the pleasure of the Lord shall prosper in his hand. He shall see of the travail of his soul, and shall be satisfied: by his knowledge shall my righteous servant justify many; for he shall bear their iniquities. Therefore will I divide him a portion with the great, and he shall divide the spoil with the strong; because he hath poured out his soul unto death: and he was numbered with the transgressors; and he bare the sin of many, and made intercession for the transgressors."(NIV 1422)

Galatians 3:13+14 says, "Christ redeemed us from the curse of the law by becoming a curse for us, for it is written: "Cursed is everyone who is hung on a pole." He redeemed us in order that the blessing given to Abraham might come to the Gentiles through Christ Jesus, so that faith we might receive the promise of the Spirit."(NIV 2313)

Jesus Christ died for all of our sins at the Cross and created eternal life for us. Jesus Christ died on the Cross of Calvary in order to make an end of all transgression and sin.

These New Testament passages describe Jesus Christ as our Savior and LORD:

Ephesians 5:23 "For a husband is the head of his wife as Christ is the head of his body, the church; he gave his life to be her Savior."(KJV 1276)

2 Peter 1:1 "This letter is from Simon Peter, a slave and apostle of Jesus Christ. I am writing to all of you who share the same precious faith we have, faith given to us by Jesus Christ, our God and Savior, who makes us right with God."(KJV 1325)

John 1:1-33 "In the beginning was the Word, and the Word was with God, and the Word was God... All things were made by him; and without him was not any thing made that was made."(KJV 1148)

Jesus Christ has come to planet Earth to give the Eternal Light of Eternal Salvation to every person who will call on His Name during the time of Christmas by saying the simple phrase "Merry Christmas" This phrase contains the Infinite Name of Christ that has the Power of Infinite Salvation for all souls that would like to live forever in heaven easily. The Holy Bible says that Jesus Christ has given Light to all mankind through the kindness of His heart. The Infinite Blood of Jesus Christ Save Souls Forever. John 1:1-50 says, "In the beginning was the Word, and the Word was with God, and the Word was God. The same was in the beginning with God. All things were made by him; and without him was not any thing made that was made. In him was life; and the life was the light of men. And the light shineth in darkness; and the darkness comprehended it not. There was a man sent from God, whose name was John. The same came for a witness, to bear witness of the Light, that all men through him might believe. He was not that Light, but was sent to bear witness of that Light. That was the true Light, which lighteth every man that cometh into the world. He was in the world, and the world was made by him, and the world knew him not. He came unto his own, and his own received him not. But as many as received him, to them gave he power to become the sons of God, even to them that believe on his name: Which were born, not of blood, nor of the will of the flesh, nor of the will of man, but of God. And the Word was made flesh, and dwelt among us, (and we beheld his glory, the glory as of the only begotten of the Father,) full of grace and truth. John bare witness of him, and cried, saying, This was he of whom I spake, He that cometh after me is preferred before me: for he was before me. And of his fulness have all we received, and grace for grace. For the law was given by Moses, but grace and truth came by Jesus Christ. No man hath seen God at any time, the only begotten Son, which is in the bosom of the Father, he hath declared him. And this is the record of John, when the Jews sent priests and Levites from Jerusalem to ask him, Who art thou? And he confessed, and denied not; but confessed, I am not the Christ. And they asked him, What then? Art thou Elias? And he saith, I am not. Art thou that prophet? And he answered, No. Then said they unto him, Who art thou? that we may give an answer to them that sent us. What sayest thou of thyself? He said, I am the voice of one crying in the wilderness,

Make straight the way of the Lord, as said the prophet Esaias. And they which were sent were of the Pharisees. And they asked him, and said unto him, Why baptizest thou then, if thou be not that Christ, nor Elias, neither that prophet? John answered them, saying, I baptize with water: but there standeth one among you, whom ye know not; He it is, who coming after me is preferred before me, whose shoe's latchet I am not worthy to unloose. These things were done in Bethabara beyond Jordan, where John was baptizing. The next day John seeth Jesus coming unto him, and saith, Behold the Lamb of God, which taketh away the sin of the world. This is he of whom I said, After me cometh a man which is preferred before me: for he was before me. And I knew him not: but that he should be made manifest to Israel, therefore am I come baptizing with water. And John bare record, saying, I saw the Spirit descending from heaven like a dove, and it abode upon him. And I knew him not: but he that sent me to baptize with water, the same said unto me, Upon whom thou shalt see the Spirit descending, and remaining on him, the same is he which baptizeth with the Holy Ghost. And I saw, and bare record that this is the Son of God. Again the next day after John stood, and two of his disciples; And looking upon Jesus as he walked, he saith, Behold the Lamb of God! And the two disciples heard him speak, and they followed Jesus. Then Jesus turned, and saw them following, and saith unto them, What seek ye? They said unto him, Rabbi, (which is to say, being interpreted, Master,) where dwellest thou? He saith unto them, Come and see. They came and saw where he dwelt, and abode with him that day: for it was about the tenth hour. One of the two which heard John speak, and followed him, was Andrew, Simon Peter's brother. He first findeth his own brother Simon, and saith unto him, We have found the Messias, which is, being interpreted, the Christ. And he brought him to Jesus. And when Jesus beheld him, he said, Thou art Simon the son of Jona: thou shalt be called Cephas, which is by interpretation, A stone. The day following Jesus would go forth into Galilee, and findeth Philip, and saith unto him, Follow me. Now Philip was of Bethsaida, the city of Andrew and Peter. Philip findeth Nathanael, and saith unto him, We have found him, of whom Moses in the law, and the prophets, did write, Jesus of Nazareth, the son of Joseph. And Nathanael said unto him, Can there any good thing come out of Nazareth? Philip saith unto him, Come and see. Jesus saw Nathanael coming to him, and saith of him, Behold an Israelite indeed, in whom is no guile! Nathanael saith unto him, Whence knowest thou me? Jesus answered and said unto him, Before that Philip called thee, when thou wast under the fig tree, I saw thee. Nathanael answered and saith unto him, Rabbi, thou art the Son of God; thou art the King of Israel. Jesus answered and said unto him, Because I said unto thee, I saw thee under the fig tree, believest thou? thou shalt see greater things than these."(KJV 1148) The Word Christ in the Word Christmas is about the eternal salvation of souls getting saved in order to have eternal life in heaven forever.

JESUS CHRIST THE CREATOR OF THE UNIVERSE

10

JESUS CHRIST IS THE CREATOR OF ALL HUMANITY BECAUSE HE MADE US

These passages describe Jesus Christ as our LORD and Creator:

Isaiah 43:3 says, "For I am the LORD, your God, the Holy One of Israel, your Savior."(KJV 799) Isaiah 43:7 declares, "Even every one that is called by my name: for I have created him for my glory, I have formed him; yea, I have made him."(KJV 799) Genesis 1:26 mentions, "And God said, 'Let us make man in our image and after our likeness.'"(KJV 2) Isaiah 43:10-11 says, "But you are my witnesses, O Israel! Says the LORD. And you are my servant. You have been chosen to know me, believe in me, and understand that I alone am God. There is no other God; there never has been and never will be. I am the LORD, and there is no other Savior."(KJV 799) Isaiah 43:15 says, "I am the LORD, your Holy One, Israel's Creator, your King."(KJV 800) Isaiah 44:6 states, "Thus saith the Lord the King of Israel, and his redeemer the Lord of hosts; I am the First and I am the Last; and beside me there is no other God."(KJV 800) Our LORD Jesus Christ is also our Rock, Redeemer, King, LORD, First, and Last.

The Holy Bible Reveals that Jesus Christ is The God of Planet Earth NOW. Revelation 1:1-20 declares, "The Revelation of Jesus Christ, which God gave unto him, to shew unto his servants things which must shortly come to pass; and he sent and signified it by his angel unto his servant John: Who bare record of the word of God, and of the testimony of Jesus Christ, and of all things that he saw. Blessed is he that readeth, and they that hear the words of this prophecy, and keep those things which are written therein: for the time is at hand. John to the seven churches which are in Asia: Grace be unto you, and peace, from him which is, and which was, and which is to come; and from the seven Spirits which are before his throne; And from Jesus Christ, who is the faithful witness, and the first begotten of the dead, and the prince of the kings of the earth. Unto him that loved us, and washed us from our sins in his own blood, And hath made us kings and priests unto God and his Father; to him be glory and dominion for ever and ever. Amen. Behold, he cometh with clouds; and every eye shall see him, and they also which pierced him: and all kindreds of the earth shall wail because of him. Even so, Amen. I am Alpha and Omega, the beginning and the ending, saith the Lord, which is, and which was, and which is to come, the Almighty. I John, who also am your brother, and companion in tribulation, and in the kingdom and patience of Jesus Christ, was in the isle that is called Patmos, for the word of God, and for the testimony of Jesus Christ. I was in the Spirit on the Lord's day, and heard behind me a great voice, as of a trumpet, Saying, I am Alpha and Omega, the first and the last: and, What thou seest, write in a book, and send it unto the seven churches which are in Asia; unto Ephesus, and unto Smyrna, and unto Pergamos, and unto Thyatira, and unto Sardis, and unto Philadelphia, and unto Laodicea. And I turned to see the voice that spake with me. And being turned, I saw seven golden candlesticks; And in the midst of the seven candlesticks one like unto the Son of man, clothed with a garment down to the foot, and girt about the paps with a golden girdle. His head and his hairs were white like wool, as white as snow; and his eyes were as a flame of fire; And his feet like unto fine brass, as if they burned in a furnace; and his voice as the sound of many waters. And he had in his right hand seven stars: and out of his mouth went a sharp twoedged sword: and his countenance was as the sun shineth in his strength. And when I saw him, I fell at his feet as dead. And he laid his right hand upon me, saying unto me, Fear not; I am the first and the last: I am he that liveth, and was dead; and, behold, I am alive for evermore, Amen; and have the keys of hell and of death. Write the things which thou hast seen, and the things which are, and the things which shall be hereafter; The mystery of the seven stars which thou sawest in my right hand, and the seven golden candlesticks. The seven stars are the angels of the seven churches: and the seven candlesticks which thou sawest are the seven churches.(KJV 1336) Here in this passage Jesus Christ says that He is the very same First and Last God that Isaiah and the other prophets wrote about in the Old Testament. Christ has the keys of eternal life.

Isaiah 44:6-8 declares, "Thus saith the LORD the King of Israel, and his redeemer the LORD of hosts; I am the first, and I am the last; and beside me there is no God. And who, as I, shall call, and shall declare it, and set it in order for me, since I appointed the ancient people? and the things that are coming, and shall come, let them shew unto them. Fear ye not, neither be afraid: have not I told thee from that time, and have declared it? ye are even my witnesses. Is there a God beside me? yea, there is no God; I know not any."(KJV 800) Isaiah 48:12-13 also says, "I alone am God, the First and the Last. It was my hand that laid the foundations of the earth. The palm of my right hand spread out the heavens above. I spoke, and they came into being."(KJV 805)

The Angel of The LORD appeared to Moses in a bright light in the midst of a Bush. Exodus 3:2 states, "the LORD appeared unto him in a flame of fire out of the midst of a bush: and he looked, and, behold, the bush burned with fire, and the bush was not consumed."(KJV 67) Jesus Christ Appeared to the Apostle Paul as a bright Light from Heaven on the Road to Damascus. Acts 9:3 "As he neared Damascus on his journey, suddenly a light from heaven flashed around him."(KJV 1192) Acts 1:8 declares, "But you will receive power when the Holy Spirit comes on you; and you will be my witnesses in Jerusalem, and in all Judea and Samaria, and to the ends of the earth."(KJV 1180)

Jesus Christ in the Bible is also the Creator, the Holy One of God, our Rock,our Lamb, & our Our King. Colossians 1:16 states, "For by him all things were created: things in heaven and on earth, visible and invisible, whether thrones or powers or rulers or authorities; all things were created by him and for him."(KJV 1282)

John the Baptist speaks of Jesus and says, The bride belongs to the bridegroom. John 3:27-30 says, "John answered and said, A man can receive nothing, except it be given him from heaven. Ye yourselves bear me witness, that I said, I am not the Christ, but that I am sent before him. He that hath the bride is the bridegroom: but the friend of the bridegroom, which standeth and heareth him, rejoiceth greatly because of the bridegroom's voice: this my joy therefore is fulfilled. He must increase"(KJV 1151) 1 Corinthians 10:4 says, "and drank the same spiritual drink; for they drank from the spiritual Rock that accompanied them, and that Rock was Christ."(NIV 2266) Revelation 19:7+16 declares, "Let us be glad and rejoice and honor him. For the time has come for the wedding feast of the Lamb, and his bride has prepared herself... his name KING OF KINGS, AND LORD OF LORDS..."(KJV 1352)

GOD + he HOLY SPIRIT

PART THREE:

God The Holy Spirit

1

THE HOLY SPIRIT IS THE CREATOR OF ALL CREATION

All things were created by the Holy Spirit working together with the pre-incarnate Angel of The LORD who would soon be born into the world and become Jesus Christ. The Holy Spirit is God Creator because the Holy Spirit is The Creator of all creation. Genesis 1:1-8 says, "In the beginning God created the heaven and the earth. And the earth was without form, and void; and darkness was upon the face of the deep. And the Spirit of God moved upon the face of the waters. And God said, Let there be light: and there was light. And God saw the light, that it was good: and God divided the light from the darkness. And God called the light Day, and the darkness he called Night. And the evening and the morning were the first day. And God said, Let there be a firmament in the midst of the waters, and let it divide the waters from the waters. And God made the firmament, and divided the waters which were under the firmament from the waters which were above the firmament: and it was so. And God called the firmament Heaven. And the evening and the morning were the second day."(KJV 1) The Holy Bible says Jesus Christ created all things in Colossians 1:16 that declares, "For by him all things were created: things in heaven and on earth, visible and invisible, whether thrones or powers or rulers or authorities; all things were created by him and for him."(KJV 1282) All things were created by the Holy Spirit of God.

THE HOLY SPIRIT CREATES THE SNOW FLAKES

2

THE HOLY SPIRIT IS THE BREATH OF LIFE

The Holy Spirit caused the breath of life to enter Adam making him a living soul in a living body together with his living spirit. Genesis 2:1-7 mentions the creation of humanity, "Thus the heavens and the earth were finished, and all the host of them. And on the seventh day God ended his work which he had made; and he rested on the seventh day from all his work which he had made. And God blessed the seventh day, and sanctified it: because that in it he had rested from all his work which God created and made. These are the generations of the heavens and of the earth when they were created, in the day that the LORD God made the earth and the heavens, And every plant of the field before it was in the earth, and every herb of the field before it grew: for the LORD God had not caused it to rain upon the earth, and there was not a man to till the ground. But there went up a mist from the earth, and watered the whole face of the ground. And the LORD God formed man of the dust of the ground, and breathed into his nostrils the breath of life; and man became a living soul."(KJV 2) The Holy Spirit is the breath of resurrection life.

The NIV Translation says that man became a living being who has a living spirit, a living soul, and a living body. Genesis 2:4-7 in the New International Version of The Holy Bible declares, "This is the account of the heavens and the earth when they were created, when the LORD God made the earth and the heavens. Now no shrub had yet appeared on the earth and no plant had yet sprung up, for the LORD God had not sent rain on the earth and there was no one to work the ground, but streams came up from the earth and watered the whole surface of the ground. Then the LORD God formed a man from the dust of the ground and breathed into his nostrils the breath of life, and the man became a living being. Now the LORD God had planted a garden in the east, in Eden; and there he put the man he had formed. The LORD God made all kinds of trees grow out of the ground trees that were pleasing to the eye and good for food. In the middle of the garden were the tree of life and the tree of the knowledge of good and evil."(NIV 9) The Holy Spirit created Adam with a Spirit from God and a Soul in Human flesh giving him a choice to choose between doing good or doing evil. The battle between the spirit and the flesh started in the first few chapters of the Holy Bible. The Holy Bible is the number one guide book on how to manage the battle of the spirit and the flesh.

THE CHRIST IN CHRISTMAS HAS INFINITE POWER TO SAVE SOULS

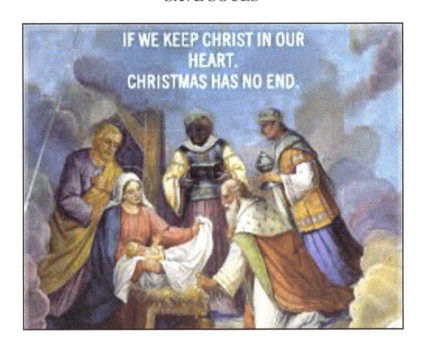

3

THE HOLY SPIRIT IN THE BIRTH OF JESUS CHRIST

The Holy Spirit of GOD lives inside of every Christian who believes in GOD. In the Holy Bible we see the Holy Spirit is the Father of Jesus Christ. The Holy Spirit of GOD also testifies that Jesus Christ died for all sin at the Cross. The Holy Spirit caused the Virgin Mary to conceive and give birth to a Son sho is called The Holy One. The Holy One born of the union of the Virgin Mary and The Holy Spirit is called The Holy One of God and this person is Jesus Christ Himself. The Holy One is The Son of The Holy Spirit. Luke 1:35 says, "The angel answered, "The Holy Spirit will come upon you, and the power of the Most High will overshadow you. So The Holy One to be born will be called the Son of God."(KJV 1105) (The Angel Gabriel Speaking to Mary)

An angel in Joseph's dream told Joseph that the Holy Spirit caused The Virgin Mary to conceive Jesus Christ in her womb and Jesus will save his people from their sins and therefore remove all sin 100%. Matthews 1:18-21 records, "Now the birth of Jesus Christ was on this wise: When as his mother Mary was espoused to Joseph, before they came together, she was found with child of the Holy Ghost. Then Joseph her husband, being a just man, and not willing to make her a public example, was minded to put her away privily. But while he thought on these things, behold, the angel of the LORD appeared unto him in a dream, saying, Joseph, thou son of David, fear not to take unto thee Mary thy wife: for that which is conceived in her is of the Holy Ghost. And she shall bring forth a son, and thou shalt call his name JESUS: for he shall save his people from their sins."(KJV 1037) Isaiah prophecies the birth of the Christ Child in Isaiah 9:6 that prophesies, " For to us a child is born, to us a son is given, and the government will be on his shoulders. And he will be called Wonderful Counselor, Mighty God, Everlasting Father, Prince of Peace."(KJV 768) Jesus Christ also existed before Abraham because John 8:58 says, "Jesus said unto them, Verily, verily, I say unto you, Before Abraham was, I am."(KJV 1161) Jesus Christ saw the day when Abraham walked on planet earth.

All Christians agree that Jesus Christ is God and also is the Savior who has saved them from their sins. Luke 1:26-48 sustains, "And in the sixth month the angel Gabriel was sent from God unto a city of Galilee, named Nazareth, To a virgin espoused to a man whose name was Joseph, of the house of David; and the virgin's name was Mary. And the angel came in unto her, and said, Hail, thou that art highly favoured, the Lord is with thee: blessed art thou among women. And when she saw him, she was troubled at his saying, and cast in her mind what manner of salutation this should be. And the angel said unto her, Fear not, Mary: for thou hast found favour with God. And, behold, thou shalt conceive in thy womb, and bring forth a son, and shalt call his name JESUS. He shall be great, and shall be called the Son of the Highest: and the Lord God shall give unto him the throne of his father David: And he shall reign over the house of Jacob for ever; and of his kingdom there shall be no end. Then said Mary unto the angel, How shall this be, seeing I know not a man? And the angel answered and said unto her, The Holy Ghost shall come upon thee, and the power of the Highest shall overshadow thee: therefore also that holy thing which shall be born of thee shall be called the Son of God. And, behold, thy cousin Elisabeth, she hath also conceived a son in her old age: and this is the sixth month with her, who was called barren. For with God nothing shall be impossible. And Mary said, Behold the handmaid of the Lord; be it unto me according to thy word. And the angel departed from her. And Mary arose in those days, and went into the hill country with haste, into a city of Juda; And entered into the house of Zacharias, and saluted Elisabeth. And it came to pass, that, when Elisabeth heard the salutation of Mary, the babe leaped in her womb; and Elisabeth was filled with the Holy Ghost: And she spake out with a loud voice, and said, Blessed art thou among women, and blessed is the fruit of thy womb. And whence is this to me, that the mother of my Lord should come to me? For, lo, as soon as the voice of thy salutation sounded in mine ears, the babe leaped in my womb for joy. And blessed is she that believed: for there shall be a performance of those things which were told her from the Lord. And Mary said, My soul doth magnify the Lord, And my spirit hath rejoiced in God my Saviour. For he hath regarded the low estate of his handmaiden: for, behold, from henceforth all generations shall call me blessed."(KJV 1105) All generations shall call me blessed because the Holy Bible says so.

Jesus Christ is the Son of the Holy Spirit. The Holy Spirit is therefore the Father of Jesus Christ. Adam was also the son of God because Luke 3:38 declares, "Which was the son of Enos, which was the son of Seth, which was the son of Adam, which was the son of God."(KJV 1110) The Father and Creator of Adam was God Himself. God the Father, God the Son in the Pre-incarnate Christ in the Angel of the LORD, And God The Holy Spirit were all three involved in The Creation of Adam. Genesis 1:26-27 says, "And God said, Let us make man in our image, after our likeness: and let them have dominion over the fish of the sea, and over the fowl of the air, and over the cattle, and over all the earth, and over every creeping thing that creepeth upon the earth. So God created man in his own image, in the image of God created he him; male and female created he them."(KJV 2)

4

THE HOLY SPIRIT HELPS TO MAKE US SONS AND DAUGHTERS OF GOD

The Sons of God are revealed upon planet earth more and more. Jesus Christ has made those who believe in Him as Savior and LORD Sons and Daughters of God. The Son of God created many Sons of God. 1 John 3:1-12 gives this Revelation that says, "Behold, what manner of love the Father hath bestowed upon us, that we should be called the Sons of God: therefore the world knoweth us not, because it knew him not. Beloved, now are we the sons of God, and it doth not yet appear what we shall be: but we know that, when he shall appear, we shall be like him; for we shall see him as he is. And every man that hath this hope in him purifieth himself, even as he is pure. Whosoever committeth sin transgresseth also the law: for sin is the transgression of the law. And ye know that he was manifested to take away our sins; and in him is no sin. Whosoever abideth in him sinneth not: whosoever sinneth hath not seen him, neither known him. Little children, let no man deceive you: he that doeth righteousness is righteous, even as he is righteous. He that committeth sin is of the devil; for the devil sinneth from the beginning. For this purpose the Son of God was manifested, that he might destroy the works of the devil. Whosoever is born of God doth not commit sin; for his seed remaineth in him: and he cannot sin, because he is born of God. In this the children of God are manifest, and the children of the devil: whosoever doeth not righteousness is not of God, neither he that loveth not his brother. For this is the message that ye heard from the beginning, that we should love one another. Not as Cain, who was of that wicked one, and slew his brother. And wherefore slew he him? Because his own works were evil, and his brother's righteous."(KJV 1329) The people who choose to receive Jesus Christ and His Teachings now become the actual children of God the Father like Jesus Christ our Big Brother.

We are Sons of God just like Jesus Christ is the Son of God in a very similar way. The Holy Spirit becomes your Father when He gives you His Spirit and saves your soul from eternal corruption in the lake of fire. The Holy Spirit renews your soul and spirit man in order to connect with Him better because He is The Holy Spirit of God and God Himself. If we are Sons and Daughters of The Holy Spirit and Jesus Christ we are also Sons and Daughters of God Himself.

The amazing power of the Holy Bible shows that Jesus Christ is the Son of God God God in 1 John 4:11-17 that proclaims, "Beloved, if God so loved us, we ought also to love one another. No man hath seen God at any time. If we love one another, God dwelleth in us, and his love is perfected in us. Hereby know we that we dwell in him, and he in us, because he hath given us of his Spirit. And we have seen and do testify that the Father sent the Son to be the Saviour of the world. Whosoever shall confess that Jesus is the Son of God, God dwelleth in him, and he in God. And we have known and believed the love that God hath to us. God is love; and he that dwelleth in love dwelleth in God, and God in him. Herein is our love made perfect, that we may have boldness in the day of judgment: because as he is, so are we in this world."(KJV 1331) = (GOD + GOD + GOD in 1 Sentence)

THE HOLY SPIRIT WORKS WITH THE SON AND THE FATHER

5

THE HOLY SPIRIT APPEARS WITH THE FATHER AND THE SON

The Holy Spirit descends upon Jesus Christ and God the Father Speaks from the clouds of Heaven. Matthew 3:16+17 proclaims, "As soon as Jesus was baptized, he went up out of the water. At that moment heaven was opened, and he saw the Spirit of God descending like a dove and lighting on him. And a voice from heaven said, 'This is my Son, whom I love; with him I am well pleased."(KJV 1039) The same Holy Spirit Dove is seen in Mark 1:9-11 that says, "At that time Jesus came from Nazareth in Galilee and was baptized by John in the Jordan. As Jesus was coming up out of the water, he saw heaven being torn open and the Spirit descending on him like a dove. And a voice came from heaven: 'You are my Son, whom I love; with you I am well pleased.'"(KJV 1078) Luke records the Holy Spirit in Luke 3:21-22 that declares, "When all the people were being baptized, Jesus was baptized too. And as he was praying, heaven was opened and the Holy Spirit descended on him in bodily form like a dove. And a voice came from heaven: "You are my Son, whom I love; with you I am well pleased."(KJV 1109) The Apostle John also give his account in John 1:32-34 that states, "Then John gave this testimony: 'I saw the Spirit come down from heaven as a dove and remain on him. I would not have known him, except that the one who sent me to baptize with water told me, The man on whom you see the Spirit come down and remain is he who will baptize with the Holy Spirit.'"(KJV 1148) John also records the heavens opening in John 1:50+51 declares, "Jesus said, 'I tell you the truth, you shall see heaven open, and the angels of God ascending and descending on the Son of Man.'"(KJV 1149) The Holy Spirit was very evident in the Ministry of Jesus Christ.

The Heavenly Father appears from heaven with Moses and Elijah to confirm that Jesus Christ is His Beloved Son again. The Holy Spirit is already upon The Ministry of Jesus Christ working in Him by The Power of The Holy Spirit. Luke 9:32-37 says, "But Peter and they that were with him were heavy with sleep: and when they were awake, they saw his glory, and the two men that stood with him.

And it came to pass, as they departed from him, Peter said unto Jesus, Master, it is good for us to be here: and let us make three tabernacles; one for thee, and one for Moses, and one for Elias: not knowing what he said. While he thus spake, there came a cloud, and overshadowed them: and they feared as they entered into the cloud. And there came a voice out of the cloud, saying, This is my beloved Son: hear him. And when the voice was past, Jesus was found alone. And they kept it close, and told no man in those days any of those things which they had seen. And it came to pass, that on the next day, when they were come down from the hill, much people met him."(KJV 1121) This was a very supernatural event that shows these men are alive.

6

THE HOLY SPIRIT DESCENDS UPON THE CHRIST OF GOD

The Gospel of Luke teaches us about the Holy Spirit of God. Luke 3:21+22 says, "When all the people were being baptized, Jesus was baptized too. And as he was praying, heaven was opened and the Holy Spirit descended on him in bodily form like a dove. And a voice came from heaven: 'You are my Son, whom I love; with you I am well pleased.'"(KJV 1109) The Holy Spirit is the Counselor and Teacher that teaches you what you ought to say because He is God. Luke 12:12 says, "the Holy Spirit will teach you at that time what you should say."(KJV 1126) The Holy Spirit gives power to His disciples to preach with power. Acts 1:8 proclaims, "But you will receive power when the Holy Spirit comes on you; and you will be my witnesses in Jerusalem, and in all Judea and Samaria, and to the ends of the earth."(KJV 1180)

THE BAPTISM OF CHRIST

7

JOHN THE BAPTIST BAPTIZES JESUS CHRIST IN THE HOLY SPIRIT

John The Baptist Baptizes Jesus Christ into the Holy Spirit's Power. Jesus Christ needed no repentance because he had no sin so John The Baptist Baptized Jesus Christ into the Baptism of The Holy Spirit Fire Power of The Holy Spirit working in The Ministry of Jesus Christ. Matthew 3:9-15 declares, "And think not to say within yourselves, We have Abraham to our father: for I say unto you, that God is able of these stones to raise up children unto Abraham. And now also the axe is laid unto the root of the trees: therefore every tree which bringeth not forth good fruit is hewn down, and cast into the fire. I indeed baptize you with water unto repentance. but he that cometh after me is mightier than I, whose shoes I am not worthy to bear: he shall baptize you with the Holy Ghost, and with fire: Whose fan is in his hand, and he will throughly purge his floor, and gather his wheat into the garner; but he will burn up the chaff with unquenchable fire. Then cometh Jesus from Galilee to Jordan unto John, to be baptized of him. But John forbad him, saying, I have need to be baptized of thee, and comest thou to me? And Jesus answering said unto him, Suffer it to be so now: for thus it becometh us to fulfil all righteousness. Then he suffered him."(KJV 1039) The Heavenly Father spoke from the Clouds of Heaven as The Holy Spirit Appeared as a Dove. The Heavenly Father speaking from Heaven is also seen and heard calling Jesus Christ His Son. Matthew 3:16-17 shows, "And Jesus, when he was baptized, went up straightway out of the water: and, lo, the heavens were opened unto him, and he saw the Spirit of God descending like a dove, and lighting upon him: And lo a voice from heaven, saying, This is my beloved Son, in whom I am well pleased."(KJV 1039) God the Father is very well pleased with His Son.

During the baptism of John the Baptist the Holy Spirit of God came upon Jesus Christ as an example unto us so that we as Christians may also be fully empowered by the Holy Spirit of God to carry on the works of God and the preaching of the Gospel. Every Christian is empowered by the Holy Spirit of God to carry out the works of God even as Jesus Christ showed us the greatest example of a life fully filled with the Holy Spirit Gifts in operation. An individual who has the Holy Spirit Gifts of God fully operating in their life accomplishes great things in the Kingdom of God.

8

THE HOLY SPIRIT HELPS JESUS CHRIST DEFEAT THE DEVIL 100%

The Holy Spirit Guided Jesus Christ into the Wilderness to be tempted by The Devil and gave him complete triumph over all the power of The Devil. Matthew 4:1-11 states, "Then was Jesus led up of the Spirit into the wilderness to be tempted of the devil. And when he had fasted forty days and forty nights, he was afterward an hungred. And when the tempter came to him, he said, If thou be the Son of God, command that these stones be made bread. But he answered and said, It is written, Man shall not live by bread alone, but by every word that proceedeth out of the mouth of God. Then the devil taketh him up into the holy city, and setteth him on a pinnacle of the temple, And saith unto him, If thou be the Son of God, cast thyself down: for it is written, He shall give his angels charge concerning thee: and in their hands they shall bear thee up, lest at any time thou dash thy foot against a stone. Jesus said unto him, It is written again, Thou shalt not tempt the Lord thy God. Again, the devil taketh him up into an exceeding high mountain, and sheweth him all the kingdoms of the world, and the glory of them; And saith unto him, All these things will I give thee, if thou wilt fall down and worship me. Then saith Jesus unto him, Get thee hence, Satan: for it is written, Thou shalt worship the Lord thy God, and him only shalt thou serve. Then the devil leaveth him, and, behold, angels came and ministered unto him."(KJV 1040) The Devil has left planet earth 100 Percent because of the power of blood of Jesus Christ. It is done.

The Devil is going to leave planet Earth 100 Percent and the Holy Angels and Saints of God will come back to planet Earth to reign and rule with Jesus Christ for 1000 years. Revelation 20:1-6 says, "And I saw an angel come down from heaven, having the key of the bottomless pit and a great chain in his hand. And he laid hold on the dragon, that old serpent, which is the Devil, and Satan, and bound him a thousand years, And cast him into the bottomless pit, and shut him up, and set a seal upon him, that he should deceive the nations no more, till the thousand years should be fulfilled: and after that he must be loosed a little season. And I saw thrones, and they sat upon them, and judgment was given unto them:

and I saw the souls of them that were beheaded for the witness of Jesus, and for the word of God, and which had not worshipped the beast, neither his image, neither had received his mark upon their foreheads, or in their hands; and they lived and reigned with Christ a thousand years. But the rest of the dead lived not again until the thousand years were finished. This is the first resurrection. Blessed and holy is he that hath part in the first resurrection: on such the second death hath no power, but they shall be priests of God and of Christ, and shall reign with him a thousand years."(KJV 1353) Some people will live 1000 years on planet earth.

The LORD Jesus Christ by the Power of The Holy Spirit has already 100 Percent overcome 100 percent all the power of sin, evil, curses, wickedness, darkness, sorcery, witchcraft, flesh, lies, deception, addiction, rebellion, bondage, slavery, sickness, disease, infirmity, and all other consequences and results of sin. The Blood of Jesus Christ at The Cross of Calvary has already completed the work 100 Percent. Revelation 16:17 says, "IT IS DONE."(KJV 1349) All the power of sin is already finished 100 Percent because John 19:30 says, "It is finished."(KJV 1176) Revelation 21:1-10 proclaims, "And I saw a new heaven and a new earth: for the first heaven and the first earth were passed away; and there was no more sea. And I John saw the holy city, new Jerusalem, coming down from God out of heaven, prepared as a bride adorned for her husband. And I heard a great voice out of heaven saying, Behold, the tabernacle of God is with men, and he will dwell with them, and they shall be his people, and God himself shall be with them, and be their God. And God shall wipe away all tears from their eyes; and there shall be no more death, neither sorrow, nor crying, neither shall there be any more pain: for the former things are passed away. And he that sat upon the throne said, Behold, I make all things new. And he said unto me, Write: for these words are true and faithful. And he said unto me, It is done. I am Alpha and Omega, the beginning and the end. I will give unto him that is athirst of the fountain of the water of life freely. He that overcometh shall inherit all things; and I will be his God, and he shall be my son. But the fearful, and unbelieving, and the abominable, and murderers, and whoremongers, and sorcerers, and idolaters, and all liars, shall have their part in the lake which burneth with fire and brimstone: which is the second death. And there came unto me one of the seven angels which had the seven vials full of the seven last plagues, and talked with me, saying, Come hither, I will shew thee the bride, the Lamb's wife. And he carried me away in the spirit to a great and high mountain, and shewed me that great city, the holy Jerusalem, descending out of heaven from God."(KJV 1353) The Holy Spirit's Holy Angels minister to Jesus Christ. The Holy Spirit is invisible and the Holy Angels are invisible also. So the Holy Spirit works together with the invisible Holy Angels to remove the invisible evil spirits out of planet earth and out of the lives of all Christians 100 Percent.

THE HOLY SPIRIT ON THE DAY OF PENTECOST IN ACTS

9

THE HOLY SPIRIT IS OUR COUNSELOR, TEACHER, AND HELPER

The Holy Spirit of God is a Person who is our Counselor, Teacher, and Helper:

John 14:26 "But the Counselor, the Holy Spirit, whom the Father will send in my name, will teach you all things and will remind you of everything I have said"(KJV 1170)

Isaiah 9:6 "For to us a child is born, to us a son is given, and the government will be on his shoulders. And he will be called Wonderful Counselor, Mighty God, Everlasting Father, Prince of Peace."

John 15:26 "When the Counselor comes, whom I will send to you from the Father, the Holy Spirit of truth who goes out from the Father, He will testify about me."(KJV 1171)

John 14:16+17 "And I will ask the Father, and He will give you another Counselor to be with you forever, the Holy Spirit of truth"(1170)

John 15:26 "When the Counselor comes, whom I will send to you from the Father, the Holy Spirit of truth who goes out from the Father, He will testify about me."(KJV 1171)

John 16:7 "But I tell you the truth: It is for your own good that I am going away. Unless I go away, the Counselor will not come to you; but if I go, I will send Him to you."(KJV 1172)

John 17:1 "Father the time has come, Glorify your Son"(KJV 1173)

John 16:13 "But when He, the Holy Spirit of truth, comes He will guide you into all truth"(KJV 1172)

1 John 2:20 "But you have an anointing from the Holy One"(KJV 1329)

Romans 8:26 "the Holy Spirit helps us…"(KJV 1230)

Acts 13:2-3 "One day as these men were worshiping the Lord and fasting, the Holy Spirit said, "Dedicate Barnabas and Saul for the special work I have for them."(KJV 1198)

10

THE HOLY SPIRIT IN THE BOOK OF ROMANS

The Apostle Paul agrees that the grace of God has more power than sin and therefore all sin is erased 100 Percent. Romans 5:19-9:33 "For as by one man's disobedience many were made sinners, so by the obedience of one shall many be made righteous. Moreover the law entered, that the offence might abound. But where sin abounded, grace did much more abound: That as sin hath reigned unto death, even so might grace reign through righteousness unto eternal life by Jesus Christ our Lord. What shall we say then? Shall we continue in sin, that grace may abound? ²God forbid. How shall we, that are dead to sin, live any longer therein? Know ye not, that so many of us as were baptized into Jesus Christ were baptized into his death? Therefore we are buried with him by baptism into death: that like as Christ was raised up from the dead by the glory of the Father, even so we also should walk in newness of life. For if we have been planted together in the likeness of his death, we shall be also in the likeness of his resurrection: Knowing this, that our old man is crucified with him, that the body of sin might be destroyed, that henceforth we should not serve sin. For he that is dead is freed from sin. Now if we be dead with Christ, we believe that we shall also live with him: Knowing that Christ being raised from the dead dieth no more; death hath no more dominion over him. For in that he died, he died unto sin once: but in that he liveth, he liveth unto God. Likewise reckon ye also yourselves to be dead indeed unto sin, but alive unto God through Jesus Christ our Lord. Let not sin therefore reign in your mortal body, that ye should obey it in the lusts thereof. Neither yield ye your members as instruments of unrighteousness unto sin: but yield yourselves unto God, as those that are alive from the dead, and your members as instruments of righteousness unto God. For sin shall not have dominion over you: for ye are not under the law, but under grace. What then? shall we sin, because we are not under the law, but under grace? God forbid. Know ye not, that to whom ye yield yourselves servants to obey, his servants ye are to whom ye obey; whether of sin unto death, or of obedience unto righteousness? But God be thanked, that ye were the servants of sin, but ye have obeyed from the heart that form of doctrine which was delivered you. Being then made free from sin, ye became the servants of righteousness. I speak after the manner of men because of the infirmity of your flesh: for as ye have yielded your members servants to uncleanness and to iniquity unto iniquity; even so now yield your members servants to righteousness unto holiness. For when ye were the servants of sin, ye were free from righteousness. What fruit had ye then in those things whereof ye are now ashamed? for the end of those things is death. But now being made free from sin, and become servants to God, ye have your fruit unto holiness, and the end everlasting life. For the wages of sin is death; but the gift of God is eternal life through Jesus Christ our Lord. Know ye not, brethren, (for I speak to them that know the law,) how that the law hath dominion over a man as long as he liveth? For the woman which hath an husband is bound by the law to her husband so long as he liveth; but if the husband be dead, she is loosed from the law of her husband. So then if, while her husband liveth, she be married to another man, she shall be called an adulteress: but if her husband be dead, she is free from that law; so that she is no adulteress, though she be married to another man. Wherefore, my brethren, ye also are become dead to the law by the body of Christ; that ye should be married to another, even to him who is raised from the dead, that we should bring forth fruit unto God. For when we were in the flesh, the motions of sins, which were by the law, did work in our members to bring forth fruit unto death. But now we are delivered from the law, that being dead wherein we were held; that we should serve in newness of spirit, and not in the oldness of the letter. What shall we say then? Is the law sin? God forbid. Nay, I had not known sin, but by the law: for I had not known lust, except the law had said, Thou shalt not covet. But sin, taking occasion by the commandment, wrought in me all manner of concupiscence. For without the law sin was dead. For I was alive without the law once: but when the commandment came, sin revived, and I died. And the commandment, which was ordained to life, I found to be unto death. For sin, taking occasion by the commandment, deceived me, and by it slew me. Wherefore the law is holy, and the commandment holy, and just, and good. Was then that which is good made death unto me? God forbid. But sin, that it might appear sin, working death in me by that which is good; that sin by the commandment might become exceeding sinful. For we know that the law is spiritual: but I am carnal, sold under sin. For that which I do I allow not: for what I would, that do I not; but what I hate, that do I. If then I do that which I would not, I consent unto the law that it is good. Now then it is no more I that do it, but sin that dwelleth in me. For I know that in me (that is, in my flesh,) dwelleth no good thing: for to will is present with me; but how to perform that which is good I find not. For the good that I would I do not: but the evil which I would not, that I do. Now if I do that I would not, it is no more I that do it, but sin that dwelleth in me. I find then a law, that, when I would do good, evil is present with me. For I delight in the law of God after the inward man: But I see another law in my members, warring against the law of my mind, and bringing me into captivity to the law of sin which is in my members. O wretched man that I am! who shall deliver me from the body of this death? I thank God through Jesus Christ our Lord. So then with the mind I myself serve the law of God; but with the flesh the law of sin. There is therefore now no condemnation to them which are in Christ Jesus, who walk not after the flesh, but after the Spirit. For the law of the Spirit of life in Christ Jesus hath made me free from the law of sin and death. For what the law could not do, in that it was weak through the flesh, God sending his own Son in the likeness of sinful flesh, and for sin, condemned sin in the flesh: That the righteousness of the law might be fulfilled in us, who walk not after the flesh, but after the Spirit. For they that are after the flesh do mind the things of the flesh; but they that are after the Spirit the things of the Spirit. For to be carnally minded is death; but to be spiritually minded is life and peace. Because the carnal mind is enmity against God: for it is not subject to the law of God, neither indeed can be. So then they that are in the flesh cannot please God. But ye are not in the flesh, but in the Spirit, if so be that the Spirit of God dwell in you. Now if any man have not the Spirit of Christ, he is none of his. And if Christ be in you, the body is dead because of sin; but the Spirit is life because of righteousness. But if the Spirit of him that raised up Jesus from the dead dwell in you, he that raised up Christ from the dead shall also quicken your mortal bodies by his Spirit that dwelleth in you. Therefore, brethren, we are debtors, not to the flesh, to live after the flesh. For if ye live after the flesh, ye shall die: but if ye through the Spirit do mortify the deeds of the body, ye shall live. For as many as are led by the Spirit of God, they are the sons of God. For ye have not received the spirit of bondage again to fear; but ye have received the Spirit of adoption, whereby we cry, Abba, Father. The Spirit itself beareth witness with our spirit, that we are the children of God: And if children, then heirs; heirs of God, and joint-heirs with Christ; if so be that we suffer with him, that we may be also glorified together. For I reckon that the sufferings of this present time are not worthy to be compared with the glory which shall be revealed in us. For the earnest expectation of the creature waiteth for the manifestation of the sons of God. For the creature was made subject to vanity, not willingly, but by reason of him who hath subjected the same in hope, Because the creature itself also shall be delivered from the bondage of corruption into the glorious liberty of the children of God. For we know that the whole creation groaneth and travaileth in pain together until now. And not only they, but ourselves also, which have the firstfruits of the Spirit, even we ourselves groan within ourselves, waiting for the adoption, to wit, the redemption of our body. For we are saved by hope: but hope that is seen is not hope: for what a man seeth, why doth he yet hope for? But if we hope for that we see not, then do we with patience wait for it. Likewise the Spirit also helpeth our infirmities: for we know not what we should pray for as we ought: but the Spirit itself maketh intercession for us with groanings which cannot be uttered. And he that searcheth the hearts knoweth what is the mind of the Spirit, because he maketh intercession for the saints according to the will of God. And we know that all things work together for good to them that love God, to them who are the called according to his purpose. For whom he did foreknow, he also did predestinate to be conformed to the image of his Son, that he might be the firstborn among many brethren. Moreover whom he did predestinate, them he also called: and whom he called, them he also justified: and whom he justified, them he also glorified. What shall we then say to these things? If God be for us, who can be against us? He that spared not his own Son, but delivered him up for us all, how shall he not with him also freely give us all things? Who shall lay any thing to the charge of God's elect? It is God that justifieth. Who is he that condemneth? It is Christ that died, yea rather, that is risen again, who is even at the right hand of God, who also maketh intercession for us. Who shall separate us from the love of Christ? shall tribulation, or distress, or persecution, or famine, or nakedness, or peril, or sword? As it is written, For thy sake we are killed all the day long; we are accounted as sheep for the slaughter. Nay, in all these things we are more than conquerors through him that loved us. For I am persuaded, that neither death, nor life, nor angels, nor principalities, nor powers, nor things present, nor things to come, Nor height, nor depth, nor any other creature, shall be able to separate us from the love of God, which is in Christ Jesus our Lord. I say the truth in Christ, I lie not, my conscience also bearing me witness in the Holy Ghost, That I have great heaviness and continual sorrow in my heart. For I could wish that myself were accursed from Christ for my brethren, my kinsmen according to the flesh: Who are Israelites; to whom pertaineth the adoption, and the glory, and the covenants, and the giving of the law, and the service of God, and the promises; Whose are the fathers, and of whom as concerning the flesh Christ came, who is over all, God blessed for ever. Amen. Not as though the word of God hath taken none effect. For they are not all Israel, which are of Israel: Neither, because they are the seed of Abraham, are they all children: but, In Isaac shall thy seed be called. That is, They which are the children of the flesh, these are not the children of God: but the children of the promise are counted for the seed. For this is the word of promise, At this time will I come, and Sarah shall have a son. And not only this; but when Rebecca also had conceived by one, even by our father Isaac; (For the children being not yet born, neither having done any good or evil, that the purpose of God according to election might stand, not of works, but of him that calleth;) It was said unto her, The elder shall serve the younger. As it is written, Jacob have I loved, but Esau have I hated. What shall we say then? Is there unrighteousness with God? God forbid. For he saith to Moses, I will have mercy on whom I will have mercy, and I will have compassion on whom I will have compassion. So then it is not of him that willeth, nor of him that runneth, but of God that sheweth mercy. For the scripture saith unto Pharaoh, Even for this same purpose have I raised thee up, that I might shew my power in thee, and that my name might be declared throughout all the earth. Therefore hath he mercy on whom he will have mercy, and whom he will he hardeneth. Thou wilt say then unto me, Why doth he yet find fault? For who hath resisted his will? Nay but, O man, who art thou that repliest against God? Shall the thing formed say to him that formed it, Why hast thou made me thus? Hath not the potter power over the clay, of the same lump to make one vessel unto honour, and another unto dishonour? What if God, willing to shew his wrath, and to make his power known, endured with much longsuffering the vessels of wrath fitted to destruction: And that he might make known the riches of his glory on the vessels of mercy, which he had afore prepared unto glory, Even us, whom he hath called, not of the Jews only, but also of the Gentiles? As he saith also in Osee, I will call them my people, which were not my people; and her beloved, which was not beloved. And it shall come to pass, that in the place where it was said unto them, Ye are not my people; there shall they be called the children of the living God. Esaias also crieth concerning Israel, Though the number of the children of Israel be as the sand of the sea, a remnant shall be saved: For he will finish the work, and cut it short in righteousness: because a short work will the Lord make upon the earth. And as Esaias said before, Except the Lord of Sabaoth had left us a seed, we had been as Sodoma, and been made like unto Gomorrha. What shall we say then? That the Gentiles, which followed not after righteousness, have attained to righteousness, even the righteousness which is of faith. But Israel, which followed after the law of righteousness, hath not attained to the law of righteousness. Wherefore? Because they sought it not by faith, but as it were by the works of the law. For they stumbled at that stumblingstone; As it is written, Behold, I lay in Sion a stumblingstone and rock of offence: and whosoever believeth on him shall not be ashamed."(KJV 1227)

> THE HOLY SPIRIT HELPS CLEANSE US OF ALL SIN 100 PERCENT BECAUSE ALL THE POWER OF SIN HAS BEEN REMOVED AND IS IN THE PAST. AS CHRISTIANS WE DO NOT NEED TO SERVE SIN BECAUSE IT IS NO LONGER OUR MASTER. THE NEW MASTER OF ALL CHRISTIANS IS JESUS CHRIST AND THEREFORE AS CHRISTIANS WE SO CHOOSE TO SERVE OUR NEW MASTER JESUS CHRIST. OUR NEW MASTER JESUS CHRIST EMPOWERS US BY THE POWER OF THE HOLY SPIRIT TO BE FREE FROM ALL THE POWER OF SIN 100 PERCENT.

Romans chapter 3 says that sins are remission and are past and therefore the power of sin does not exist anymore. Romans 3:1-29 declares, "What advantage then hath the Jew? or what profit is there of circumcision? Much every way: chiefly, because that unto them were committed the oracles of God. For what if some did not believe? shall their unbelief make the faith of God without effect? God forbid: yea, let God be true, but every man a liar; as it is written, That thou mightest be justified in thy sayings, and mightest overcome when thou art judged. But if our unrighteousness commend the righteousness of God, what shall we say? Is God unrighteous who taketh vengeance? (I speak as a man) God forbid: for then how shall God judge the world? For if the truth of God hath more abounded through my lie unto his glory; why yet am I also judged as a sinner? And not rather, (as we be slanderously reported, and as some affirm that we say,) Let us do evil, that good may come? whose damnation is just. What then? are we better than they? No, in no wise: for we have before proved both Jews and Gentiles, that they are all under sin; As it is written, There is none righteous, no, not one: There is none that understandeth, there is none that seeketh after God. They are all gone out of the way, they are together become unprofitable; there is none that doeth good, no, not one. Their throat is an open sepulchre; with their tongues they have used deceit; the poison of asps is under their lips: Whose mouth is full of cursing and bitterness: Their feet are swift to shed blood: Destruction and misery are in their ways: And the way of peace have they not known: There is no fear of God before their eyes. Now we know that what things soever the law saith, it saith to them who are under the law: that every mouth may be stopped, and all the world may become guilty before God. Therefore by the deeds of the law there shall no flesh be justified in his sight: for by the law is the knowledge of sin. But now the righteousness of God without the law is manifested, being witnessed by the law and the prophets; Even the righteousness of God which is by faith of Jesus Christ unto all and upon all them that believe: for there is no difference: For all have sinned, and come short of the glory of God; Being justified freely by his grace through the redemption that is in Christ Jesus: Whom God hath set forth to be a propitiation through faith in his blood, to declare his righteousness for the remission of sins that are past, through the forbearance of God; To declare, I say, at this time his righteousness: that he might be just, and the justifier of him which believeth in Jesus. Where is boasting then? It is excluded. By what law? of works? Nay: but by the law of faith. Therefore we conclude that a man is justified by faith without the deeds of the law. Is he the God of the Jews only? is he not also of the Gentiles? Yes, of the Gentiles also:"(KJV 1225)

THE HOLY SPIRIT HELPS US AND GUIDES US INTO ALL TRUTH

11

THE HOLY SPIRIT IN THE NAME OF JESUS CHRIST HAS ALREADY DONE AWAY WITH ALL THE POWER OF SIN AT THE CROSS OF CALVARY, IT IS DONE

James the brother of Jesus Christ agrees that sin is finished!!! WOW! The Apostle James shows that The Holy Bible Explains The Holy Bible. The Holy Bible interprets The Holy Bible. Jesus Christ's last Words on The Cross of Calvary were "It is Finished". After Jesus Christ said these words He gave up the Ghost and died for all of our sins. The Apostle James came into the realization that his brother Jesus Christ was the real Messiah after he saw Jesus Christ Resurrected from the dead. All the doubts of James and Jude the brothers of Jesus Christ were erased after they saw Him come back to life from the Cross. So the Apostle James was given the Ministry of being one of the Main Apostles along with the Apostle Peter who both met with the Apostle Paul. The Apostle Peter and the Apostle James both met with the Apostle Paul to discuss the issue of circumcision in the early church. The Holy Bible shows that God is in control of everything. The two disciples of Jesus Christ that were named James who then both became Apostles in a way were an introduction to James the brother of Jesus Christ. The two disciples of Jesus Christ named Judas also in a way introduced the Apostle Jude the brother of Jesus Christ. Both James and Jude were brothers of Jesus Christ who wrote a book of the Holy Bible to testify that Jesus Christ is the real Messiah. James shows that Jesus Christ's Words, "It is finished" were referring to how sin is finished 100 percent. It is true that all sin and all the power of sin is finished and done away with because Revelation 21:6 says, "It is done"(KJV 1355). The entire Book of Revelation says all sin is removed and done, Revelation 16:17 "It is done"(KJV 1349) John 17:4 declares, "I have glorified thee on the earth: I have finished the work which thou gavest me to do"(KJV 1173). John 19:30 proclaims, "It is finished"(KJV 1176). Luke 12:50 testifies, "It is accomplished"(KJV 1128). John 4:34 says, "My meat is to finish His work"(KJV 1153). The meat of the Lamb of God finished the Work at The Cross of Calvary 100 Percent. Yes the actual meat of Jesus Christ's Body was given to Him to perform The Work of the Cross of Calvary. Luke says all the work to remove sin has already been completed because Luke 12:50 confirms, "It is completed!"(NIV 2027) The Prophet Ezekiel agrees that sin is done away with 100 percent when he says in Ezekiel 39:8, "It is done"(KJV 946) In the NIV translation of the Holy Bible Ezekiel 39:8 prophecies, "It is coming. It will surely take place, declares The Sovereign LORD. This is The Day I have declared it"(NIV 1666). Luke 14:22 also submits, "It is done"(KJV 1130)

The Apostle James the brother of Jesus Christ also served God in Ministry as one of the pillars of the early Christian Church. James 1:1-21 declares, "James, a servant of God and of the Lord Jesus Christ, to the twelve tribes which are scattered abroad, greeting. My brethren, count it all joy when ye fall into divers temptations; Knowing this, that the trying of your faith worketh patience. But let patience have her perfect work, that ye may be perfect and entire, wanting nothing. If any of you lack wisdom, let him ask of God, that giveth to all men liberally, and upbraideth not; and it shall be given him. But let him ask in faith, nothing wavering. For he that wavereth is like a wave of the sea driven with the wind and tossed. For let not that man think that he shall receive any thing of the Lord. A double minded man is unstable in all his ways. Let the brother of low degree rejoice in that he is exalted: But the rich, in that he is made low: because as the flower of the grass he shall pass away. For the sun is no sooner risen with a burning heat, but it withereth the grass, and the flower thereof falleth, and the grace of the fashion of it perisheth: so also shall the rich man fade away in his ways. Blessed is the man that endureth temptation: for when he is tried, he shall receive the crown of life, which the Lord hath promised to them that love him. Let no man say when he is tempted, I am tempted of God: for God cannot be tempted with evil, neither tempteth he any man: But every man is tempted, when he is drawn away of his own lust, and enticed. Then when lust hath conceived, it bringeth forth sin: and sin, when it is finished, bringeth forth death. Do not err, my beloved brethren. Every good gift and every perfect gift is from above, and cometh down from the Father of lights, with whom is no variableness, neither shadow of turning. Of his own will begat he us with the word of truth, that we should be a kind of firstfruits of his creatures. Wherefore, my beloved brethren, let every man be swift to hear, slow to speak, slow to wrath: For the wrath of man worketh not the righteousness of God. Wherefore lay apart all filthiness and superfluity of naughtiness, and receive with meekness the engrafted word, which is able to save your souls."(KJV 1316) The Word Christ in Christmas is able to save the souls of billions of people in all languages.

Zechariah declares that God will remove all iniquity because the cleansing of planet earth from all sin is not by might nor by power but by The Power of The Holy Spirit. Zechariah 3:1-4:6 declares, "And he shewed me Joshua the high priest standing before the Angel of the LORD, and Satan standing at his right hand to resist him. And the LORD said unto Satan, The LORD rebuke thee, O Satan; even the LORD that hath chosen Jerusalem rebuke thee: is not this a brand plucked out of the fire? Now Joshua was clothed with filthy garments, and stood before the angel. And he answered and spake unto those that stood before him, saying, Take away the filthy garments from him. And unto him he said, Behold, I have caused thine iniquity to pass from thee, and I will clothe thee with change of raiment. And I said, Let them set a fair mitre upon his head. So they set a fair mitre upon his head, and clothed him with garments. And the angel of the LORD stood by. And the angel of the LORD protested unto Joshua, saying, Thus saith the LORD of hosts; If thou wilt walk in my ways, and if thou wilt keep my charge, then thou shalt also judge my house, and shalt also keep my courts, and I will give thee places to walk among these that stand by. Hear now, O Joshua the high priest, thou, and thy fellows that sit before thee: for they are men wondered at: for, behold, I will bring forth my servant the BRANCH. For behold the stone that I have laid before Joshua; upon one stone shall be seven eyes: behold, I will engrave the graving thereof, saith the LORD of hosts, and I will remove the iniquity of that land in one day. In that day, saith the LORD of hosts, shall ye call every man his neighbour under the vine and under the fig tree. And the angel that talked with me came again, and waked me, as a man that is wakened out of his sleep. And said unto me, What seest thou? And I said, I have looked, and behold a candlestick all of gold, with a bowl upon the top of it, and his *seven* lamps thereon, and *seven* pipes to the *seven* lamps, which are upon the top thereof: And two olive trees by it, one upon the right side of the bowl, and the other upon the left side thereof. So I answered and spake to the angel that talked with me, saying, What are these, my lord? Then the angel that talked with me answered and said unto me, Knowest thou not what these be? And I said, No, my lord. Then he answered and spake unto me, saying, This is the word of the LORD unto Zerubbabel, saying, Not by might, nor by power, but by my Spirit, saith the LORD of hosts."(KJV 1023) It is the power of the Holy Spirit that works mightily.

In the New Testament the Apostle Peter speaks about obeying God. Acts 5:29-35 states, "Then Peter and the other apostles answered and said, We ought to obey God rather than men. The God of our fathers raised up Jesus, whom ye slew and hanged on a tree. Him hath God exalted with his right hand to be a Prince and a Savior, for to give repentance to Israel, and forgiveness of sins. And we are his witnesses of these things; and so is also the Holy Ghost, whom God hath given to them that obey him. When they heard that, they were cut to the heart, and took counsel to slay them. Then stood there up one in the council, a Pharisee, named Gamaliel, a doctor of the law, had in reputation among all the people, and commanded to put the apostles forth a little space; And said unto them, Ye men of Israel, take heed to yourselves what ye intend to do as touching these men."(KJV 1186) More powers of the Holy Spirit are given to those people that obey God.

12

THE HOLY SPIRIT CLEANSES AND SANCTIFIES US INTO HOLINESS MORE AND MORE MANY TIMES CONTINUALLY

The Holy Spirit is able to cleanse us and sanctify us into Holiness more and more many times continually because of the blood of Jesus Christ. The Holy Spirit helps cleanse us of all sin 100 percent because all the power of sin has been removed and is past because sin is now in the past because we have passed from the power of sin into the power of holiness. As Christians that have been renewed by the power of the Holy Spirit we do not need to serve sin because it is no longer our master. The New Master of all Christians is Jesus Christ and therefore as Christians we have decided to choose to serve our New Master Jesus Christ. Jesus Christ by the power of the Holy Spirit empowers us to be set free in the Holy Spirit and no longer in bondage to sin. Hebrews 1:1-14 declares, "God, who at sundry times and in divers manners spake in time past unto the fathers by the prophets, Hath in these last days spoken unto us by his Son, whom he hath appointed heir of all things, by whom also he made the worlds; Who being the brightness of his glory, and the express image of his person, and upholding all things by the word of his power, when he had by himself purged our sins, sat down on the right hand of the Majesty on High: Being made so much better than the angels, as he hath by inheritance obtained a more excellent name than they. For unto which of the angels said he at any time, Thou art my Son, this day have I begotten thee? And again, I will be to him a Father, and he shall be to me a Son? And again, when he bringeth in the firstbegotten into the world, he saith, And let all the angels of God worship him. And of the angels he saith, Who maketh his angels spirits, and his ministers a flame of fire. But unto the Son he saith, Thy throne, O God, is for ever and ever: a sceptre of righteousness is the sceptre of thy kingdom. Thou hast loved righteousness, and hated iniquity; therefore God, even thy God, hath anointed thee with the oil of gladness above thy fellows. And, Thou, Lord, in the beginning hast laid the foundation of the earth; and the heavens are the works of thine hands: They shall perish; but thou remainest; and they all shall wax old as doth a garment; And as a vesture shalt thou fold them up, and they shall be changed: but thou art the same, and thy years shall not fail. But to which of the angels said he at any time, Sit on my right hand, until I make thine enemies thy footstool? Are they not all ministering spirits, sent forth to minister for them who shall be heirs of salvation?"(KJV 1303) As Christians we are to sit in heavenly places with Jesus Christ.

Now the power of the Name of Christ has been made manifest to all humanity. It may be very possible that the infinite Name of Christ potentially has enough power to save 99 percent of humanity. Revelation 12:10 declares, "And I heard a loud voice saying in heaven, Now is come salvation, and strength, and the kingdom of our God, and the power of his Christ"(KJV 1346) The power of Salvation is now come to all of planet earth.

The Apostle Peter says that since all sin has been done away with that people should lay aside all their sins and follow God and taste the LORD's infinite mercy that erases all sin 100 percent. The Words of The Apostle Peter declare that you are a holy nation and a royal priesthood. The Holy Priesthood are the Priests full of the Holy Spirit of God working in them powerfully to remove sin and cleanse the people of God into increasing higher levels of holiness. 1 Peter 2:1-25 says, "Wherefore laying aside all malice, and all guile, and hypocrisies, and envies, and all evil speakings, As newborn babes, desire the sincere milk of the word, that ye may grow thereby: If so be ye have tasted that the Lord is gracious. To whom coming, as unto a living stone, disallowed indeed of men, but chosen of God, and precious, Ye also, as lively stones, are built up a spiritual house, an holy priesthood, to offer up spiritual sacrifices, acceptable to God by Jesus Christ. Wherefore also it is contained in the scripture, Behold, I lay in Sion a chief corner stone, elect, precious: and he that believeth on him shall not be confounded. Unto you therefore which believe he is precious: but unto them which be disobedient, the stone which the builders disallowed, the same is made the head of the corner, And a stone of stumbling, and a rock of offence, even to them which stumble at the word, being disobedient: whereunto also they were appointed. But ye are a chosen generation, a royal priesthood, an holy nation, a peculiar people; that ye should shew forth the praises of him who hath called you out of darkness into his marvellous light; Which in time past were not a people, but are now the people of God: which had not obtained mercy, but now have obtained mercy. Dearly beloved, I beseech you as strangers and pilgrims, abstain from fleshly lusts, which war against the soul; Having your conversation honest among the Gentiles: that, whereas they speak against you as evildoers, they may by your good works, which they shall behold, glorify God in the day of visitation. Submit yourselves to every ordinance of man for the Lord's sake: whether it be to the king, as supreme; Or unto governors, as unto them that are sent by him for the punishment of evildoers, and for the praise of them that do well. For so is the will of God, that with well doing ye may put to silence the ignorance of foolish men: As free, and not using your liberty for a cloke of maliciousness, but as the servants of God. Honour all men. Love the brother-hood. Fear God. Honour the king. Servants, be subject to your masters with all fear; not only to the good and gentle, but also to the froward. For this is thankworthy, if a man for conscience toward God endure grief, suffering wrongfully. For what glory is it, if, when ye be buffeted for your faults, ye shall take it patiently? but if, when ye do well, and suffer for it, ye take it patiently, this is acceptable with God. For even hereunto were ye called: because Christ also suffered for us, leaving us an example, that ye should follow his steps: Who did no sin, neither was guile found in his mouth: Who, when he was reviled, reviled not again; when he suf-fered, he threatened not; but committed himself to him that judgeth righteously: Who his own self bare our sins in his own body on the tree, that we, being dead to sins, should live unto righteousness: by whose stripes ye were healed. For ye were as sheep going astray; but are now returned unto the Shepherd and Bishop of your souls."(KJV 1321) All our sins are erased 100 percent and we are sanctified in Christ more and more.

The LORD Jesus Christ by the Power of the Holy Spirit of God has brought all the power of sin to a complete end 100 Percent in the blood of Jesus Christ at the Cross. All evil spirits are removed 100 percent off of planet earth into the lake of fire in the Book of Revelation. Revelation 21:6 says "It is done."(KJV 1356) Revelation 20:1-10 also declares, "And I saw an angel come down from heaven, having the key of the bottomless pit and a great chain in his hand. And he laid hold on the dragon, that old serpent, which is the Devil, and Satan, and bound him a thousand years, And cast him into the bottomless pit, and shut him up, and set a seal upon him, that he should deceive the nations no more, till the thousand years should be fulfilled: and after that he must be loosed a little season. And I saw thrones, and they sat upon them, and judgment was given unto them: and I saw the souls of them that were beheaded for the witness of Jesus, and for the word of God, and which had not worshipped the beast, neither his image, neither had received his mark upon their foreheads, or in their hands; and they lived and reigned with Christ a thousand years. But the rest of the dead lived not again until the thousand years were finished. This is the first resurrection. Blessed and holy is he that hath part in the first resurrection: on such the second death hath no power, but they shall be priests of God and of Christ, and shall reign with him a thousand years. And when the thousand years are expired, Satan shall be loosed out of his prison, And shall go out to deceive the nations which are in the four quarters of the earth, Gog, and Magog, to gather them together to battle: the number of whom is as the sand of the sea. And they went up on the breadth of the earth, and compassed the camp of the saints about, and the beloved city: and fire came down from God out of heaven, and devoured them. And the devil that deceived them was cast into the lake of fire and brimstone, where the beast and the false prophet are, and shall be tormented day and night forever and ever."(KJV 1353) This passage shows us that in the Millennium there are going to be angel like persons on planet earth that are already in their eternal bodies. These people will live and reign with Jesus Christ 1000 years. They will minister to Jesus Christ.

King David the person that is credited for writing the book of Psalms also agrees that the wickedness of sin has come to an end because God has no pleasure in the wickedness of sin and hates iniquity. God will make sin come to an end. Psalms 5-9 maintains, "Give ear to my words, O LORD, consider my meditation. Hearken unto the voice of my cry, my King, and my God: for unto thee will I pray. My voice shalt thou hear in the morning, O LORD; in the morning will I direct my prayer unto thee, and will look up. For thou art not a God that hath pleasure in wickedness: neither shall evil dwell with thee. The foolish shall not stand in thy sight: thou hatest all workers of iniquity. Thou shalt destroy them that speak leasing: the LORD will abhor the bloody and deceitful man. But as for me, I will come into thy house in the multitude of thy mercy: and in thy fear will I worship toward thy holy temple. Lead me, O LORD, in thy righteousness because of mine enemies; make thy way straight before my face. For there is no faithfulness in their mouth; their inward part is very wickedness; their throat is an open sepulchre; they flatter with their tongue. Destroy thou them, O God; let them fall by their own counsels; cast them out in the multitude of their transgressions; for they have rebelled against thee. But let all those that put their trust in thee rejoice: let them ever shout for joy, because thou defendest them: let them also that love thy name be joyful in thee. For thou, LORD, wilt bless the righteous; with favour wilt thou compass him as with a shield. O LORD, rebuke me not in thine anger, neither chasten me in thy hot displeasure. Have mercy upon me, O LORD; for I am weak: O LORD, heal me; for my bones are vexed. My soul is also sore vexed: but thou, O LORD, how long? Return, O LORD, deliver my soul: oh save me for thy mercies' sake. For in death there is no remembrance of thee: in the grave who shall give thee thanks? I am weary with my groaning; all the night make I my bed to swim; I water my couch with my tears. Mine eye is consumed because of grief; it waxeth old because of all mine enemies. Depart from me, all ye workers of iniquity; for the LORD hath heard the voice of my weeping. The LORD hath heard my supplication; the LORD will receive my prayer. Let all mine enemies be ashamed and sore vexed: let them return and be ashamed suddenly. O LORD my God, in thee do I put my trust: save me from all them that persecute me, and deliver me: Lest he tear my soul like a lion, rending it in pieces, while there is none to deliver. O LORD my God, If I have done this; if there be iniquity in my hands; If I have rewarded evil unto him that was at peace with me; (yea, I have delivered him that without cause is mine enemy:) Let the enemy persecute my soul, and take it; yea, let him tread down my life upon the earth, and lay mine honour in the dust. Selah. Arise, O LORD, in thine anger, lift up thyself because of the rage of mine enemies: and awake for me to the judgment that thou hast commanded. So shall the congregation of the people compass thee about: for their sakes therefore return thou on high. The LORD shall judge the people: judge me, O LORD, according to my righteousness, and according to mine integrity that is in me. Oh let the wickedness of the wicked come to an end; but establish the just: for the righteous God trieth the hearts and reins. My defence is of God, which saveth the upright in heart. God judgeth the righteous, and God is angry with the wicked every day. If he turn not, he will whet his sword; he hath bent his bow, and made it ready. He hath also prepared for him the instruments of death; he ordaineth his arrows against the persecutors. Behold, he travaileth with iniquity, and hath conceived mischief, and brought forth falsehood. He made a pit, and digged it, and is fallen into the ditch which he made. His mischief shall return upon his own head, and his violent dealing shall come down upon his own pate. I will praise the LORD according to his righteousness: and will sing praise to the name of the LORD most high. O LORD, our Lord, how excellent is thy name in all the earth! who hast set thy glory above the heavens. Out of the mouth of babes and sucklings hast thou ordained strength because of thine enemies, that thou mightest still the enemy and the avenger. When I consider thy heavens, the work of thy fingers, the moon and the stars, which thou hast ordained; What is man, that thou art mindful of him? and the son of man, that thou visitest him? For thou hast made him a little lower than the angels, and hast crowned him with glory and honour. Thou madest him to have dominion over the works of thy hands; thou hast put all things under his feet: All sheep and oxen, yea, and the beasts of the field; The fowl of the air, and the fish of the sea, and whatsoever passeth through the paths of the seas. O LORD our Lord, how excellent is thy name in all the earth! I will praise thee, O LORD, with my whole heart; I will shew forth all thy marvellous works. I will be glad and rejoice in thee: I will sing praise to thy name, O thou most High. When mine enemies are turned back, they shall fall and perish at thy presence. For thou hast maintained my right and my cause; thou satest in the throne judging right. Thou hast rebuked the heathen, thou hast destroyed the wicked, thou hast put out their name for ever and ever. O thou enemy, destructions are come to a perpetual end: and thou hast destroyed cities; their memorial is perished with them. But the LORD shall endure for ever: he hath prepared his throne for judgment. And he shall judge the world in righteousness, he shall minister judgment to the people in uprightness. The LORD also will be a refuge for the oppressed, a refuge in times of trouble. And they that know thy name will put their trust in thee: for thou, LORD, hast not forsaken them that seek thee. Sing praises to the LORD, which dwelleth in Zion: declare among the people his doings. When he maketh inquisition for blood, he remembereth them: he forgetteth not the cry of the humble. Have mercy upon me, O LORD; consider my trouble which I suffer of them that hate me, thou that liftest me up from the gates of death: That I may shew forth all thy praise in the gates of the daughter of Zion: I will rejoice in thy salvation. The heathen are sunk down in the pit that they made: in the net which they hid is their own foot taken.

The LORD is known by the judgment which he executeth: the wicked is snared in the work of his own hands. Higgaion. Selah. The wicked shall be turned into hell, and all the nations that forget God. For the needy shall not always be forgotten: the expectation of the poor shall not perish for ever. Arise, O LORD; let not man prevail: let the heathen be judged in thy sight. Put them in fear, O LORD: that the nations may know themselves to be but men. Selah.(KJV 638) God shows mercy to those who ask Him for mercy.

Once people begin to cleanse themselves from sins on a continual basis they begin to walk more and more in a perfect way they begin to live with a perfect heart many many times over. Psalm 99-101 says, "The LORD reigneth; let the people tremble: he sitteth between the cherubims; let the earth be moved. The LORD is great in Zion; and he is high above all the people. Let them praise thy great and terrible name; for it is holy. The king's strength also loveth judgment; thou dost establish equity, thou executest judgment and righteousness in Jacob. Exalt ye the LORD our God, and worship at his footstool; for he is holy. Moses and Aaron among his priests, and Samuel among them that call upon his name; they called upon the LORD, and he answered them. He spake unto them in the cloudy pillar: they kept his testimonies, and the ordinance that he gave them. Thou answeredst them, O LORD our God: thou wast a God that forgavest them, though thou tookest vengeance of their inventions. Exalt the LORD our God, and worship at his holy hill; for the LORD our God is holy. Make a joyful noise unto the LORD, all ye lands. Serve the LORD with gladness: come before his presence with singing. Know ye that the LORD he is God: it is he that hath made us, and not we ourselves; we are his people, and the sheep of his pasture. Enter into his gates with thanksgiving, and into his courts with praise: be thankful unto him, and bless his name. For the LORD is good; his mercy is everlasting; and his truth endureth to all generations. I will sing of mercy and judgment: unto thee, O LORD, will I sing. I will behave myself wisely in a perfect way. O when wilt thou come unto me? I will walk within my house with a perfect heart."(KJV 690) God is a Good God who shows mercy and grace.

All the power of sin has been removed by the power of the Holy Spirit of God with the perfect blood of Jesus Christ. The blood of Jesus Christ has cleansed all people on planet from all sins. 1 John 1:1-2:3 says, "That which was from the beginning, which we have heard, which we have seen with our eyes, which we have looked upon, and our hands have handled, of the Word of life; (For the life was manifested, and we have seen it, and bear witness, and shew unto you that eternal life, which was with the Father, and was manifested unto us;) That which we have seen and heard declare we unto you, that ye also may have fellowship with us: and truly our fellowship is with the Father, and with his Son Jesus Christ. And these things write we unto you, that your joy may be full. This then is the message which we have heard of him, and declare unto you, that God is light, and in him is no darkness at all. If we say that we have fellowship with him, and walk in darkness, we lie, and do not the truth: But if we walk in the light, as he is in the light, we have fellowship one with another, and the blood of Jesus Christ his Son cleanseth us from all sin. If we say that we have no sin, we deceive ourselves, and the truth is not in us. If we confess our sins, he is faithful and just to forgive us our sins, and to cleanse us from all unrighteousness. If we say that we have not sinned, we make him a liar, and his word is not in us. My little children, these things write I unto you, that ye sin not. And if any man sin, we have an advocate with the Father, Jesus Christ the righteous: And he is the propitiation for our sins: and not for ours only, but also for the sins of the whole world. And hereby we do know that we know Him"(KJV 1328) It is clear that the blood of Jesus Christ cleanses all our sins away 100 percent.

Jesus Christ has destroyed all the works of evil by the power of the Holy Spirit of God. 1 John 3:1-9 proclaims, "Behold, what manner of love the Father hath bestowed upon us, that we should be called the sons of God: therefore the world knoweth us not, because it knew him not. Beloved, now are we the sons of God, and it doth not yet appear what we shall be: but we know that, when he shall appear, we shall be like him; for we shall see him as he is. And every man that hath this hope in him purifieth himself, even as he is pure. Whosoever committeth sin transgresseth also the law: for sin is the transgression of the law. And ye know that he was manifested to take away our sins; and in him is no sin. Whosoever abideth in him sinneth not: whosoever sinneth hath not seen him, neither known him. Little children, let no man deceive you: he that doeth righteousness is righteous, even as he is righteous. He that committeth sin is of the devil; for the devil sinneth from the beginning. For this purpose the Son of God was manifested, that he might destroy the works of the devil. Whosoever is born of God doth not commit sin; for his seed remaineth in him: and he cannot sin, because he is born of God. In this the children of God are manifest"(KJV 1329) John 15:25–17:11 also says, "But when the Comforter is come, whom I will send unto you from the Father, even the Spirit of truth, which proceedeth from the Father, he shall testify of me: And ye also shall bear witness, because ye have been with me from the beginning. These things have I spoken unto you, that ye should not be offended. They shall put you out of the synagogues: yea, the time cometh, that whosoever killeth you will think that he doeth God service. And these things will they do unto you, because they have not known the Father, nor me. But these things have I told you, that when the time shall come, ye may remember that I told you of them. And these things I said not unto you at the beginning, because I was with you. But now I go my way to him that sent me; and none of you asketh me, Whither goest thou? But because I have said these things unto you, sorrow hath filled your heart. Nevertheless I tell you the truth; It is expedient for you that I go away: for if I go not away, the Comforter will not come unto you; but if I depart, I will send him unto you. And when he is come, he will reprove the world of sin, and of righteousness, and of judgment: Of sin, because they believe not on me; Of righteousness, because I go to my Father, and ye see me no more; Of judgment, because the prince of this world is judged. I have yet many things to say unto you, but ye cannot bear them now. Howbeit when he, the Spirit of truth, is come, he will guide you into all truth: for he shall not speak of himself; but whatsoever he shall hear, that shall he speak: and he will shew you things to come. He shall glorify me: for he shall receive of mine, and shall shew it unto you. All things that the Father hath are mine: therefore said I, that he shall take of mine, and shall shew it unto you. A little while, and ye shall not see me: and again, a little while, and ye shall see me, because I go to the Father. Then said some of his disciples among themselves, What is this that he saith unto us, A little while, and ye shall not see me: and again, a little while, and ye shall see me: and, Because I go to the Father? They said therefore, What is this that he saith, A little while? we cannot tell what he saith. Now Jesus knew that they were desirous to ask him, and said unto them, Do ye enquire among yourselves of that I said, A little while, and ye shall not see me: and again, a little while, and ye shall see me? Verily, verily, I say unto you, That ye shall weep and lament, but the world shall rejoice: and ye shall be sorrowful, but your sorrow shall be turned into joy. A woman when she is in travail hath sorrow, because her hour is come: but as soon as she is delivered of the child, she remembereth no more the anguish, for joy that a man is born into the world. And ye now therefore have sorrow: but I will see you again, and your heart shall rejoice, and your joy no man taketh from you. And in that day ye shall ask me nothing. Verily, verily, I say unto you, Whatsoever ye shall ask the Father in my name, he will give it you. Hitherto have ye asked nothing in my name: ask, and ye shall receive, that your joy may be full. These things have I spoken unto you in proverbs: but the time cometh, when I shall no more speak unto you in proverbs, but I shall shew you plainly of the Father. At that day ye shall ask in my name: and I say not unto you, that I will pray the Father for you: For the Father himself loveth you, because ye have loved me, and have believed that I came out from God. I came forth from the Father, and am come into the world: again, I leave the world, and go to the Father. His disciples said unto him, Lo, now speakest thou plainly, and speakest no proverb. Now are we sure that thou knowest all things, and needest not that any man should ask thee: by this we believe that thou camest forth from God. Jesus answered them, Do ye now believe? Behold, the hour cometh, yea, is now come, that ye shall be scattered, every man to his own, and shall leave me alone: and yet I am not alone, because the Father is with me. These things I have spoken unto you, that in me ye might have peace. In the world ye shall have tribulation: but be of good cheer; I have overcome the world. These words spake Jesus, and lifted up his eyes to heaven, and said, Father, the hour is come; glorify thy Son, that thy Son also may glorify thee: As thou hast given him power over all flesh, that he should give eternal life to as many as thou hast given him. And this is life eternal, that they might know thee the only true God, and Jesus Christ, whom thou hast sent. I have glorified thee on the earth: I have finished the work which thou gavest me to do. And now, O Father, glorify thou me with thine own self with the glory which I had with thee before the world was. I have manifested thy name unto the men which thou gavest me out of the world: thine they were, and thou gavest them me; and they have kept thy word. Now they have known that all things whatsoever thou hast given me are of thee. For I have given unto them the words which thou gavest me; and they have received them, and have known surely that I came out from thee, and they have believed that thou didst send me. I pray for them: I pray not for the world, but for them which thou hast given me; for they are thine. And all mine are thine, and thine are mine; and I am glorified in them. And now I am no more in the world, but these are in the world, and I come to thee. Holy Father, keep through thine own name those whom thou hast given me, that they may be one, as we are."(KJV 1171) We are one with Jesus Christ with the Holy Spirit living inside us.

There are many new things to learn on the internet and other forums. Some of these new technologies come from companies like Google, Facebook, Microsoft, Apple, Silicon Valley, Forbes, Fortune 500, And Other Emerging New Technologies. God Bless America. Revelation 21:6 says, "It is done".

BIBLIOGRAPHY

1. Nelson, Thomas Giant Print Holy Bible King James Version. Nashville: Thomas Nelson Publishers, 2003.

2. Palmer, Edwin The NIV Study Bible. Gran Rapids, Michigan: Zondervan Publishing, 1995.

3. Strong, James Strong's Exhaustive Concordance of the Bible. Peabody, Massachsetts : Hendrickson Publishers, 1981.

4. Vine, W. E. Vine's Complete Expository Dictionary of Old and New Testament Words. Atlanta: Thomas Nelson Publishers, 1996.

5. Charts Created By Dr. Snow on Microsoft Word and PowerPoint.

6. Art From Clip Art Web Page

GOD † he FATHER
GOD † he SON
GOD † he HOLY SPIRIT

=

GOD † he FATHER
† he SON
† he HOLY SPIRIT

The Pyramid Of God

(PRINT COPY PAGE AND USE SCISSORS ON 1 BIG FOLDING PYRAMID
AND CLEAR TAPE)

DO YOU KNOW THE REASON WHY YOU ARE GOING TO HAVE ETERNAL LIFE IN HEAVEN?

GOD WANTS YOU TO KNOW THAT YOU CAN HAVE ETERNAL LIFE. THIS BOOKLET IS DESIGNED TO SHOW YOU HOW YOU CAN LIVE FOREVER IN HEAVEN.
1 JOHN 5:13 "THESE THINGS I HAVE WRITTEN UNTO YOU THAT BELIEVE ON THE NAME OF THE SON OF GOD THAT YE MAY KNOW THAT YE HAVE ETERNAL LIFE THAT YE MAY BELIEVE ON THE NAME OF THE SON OF GOD."
EPHESIANS 3:9 "AND TO MAKE ALL MEN SEE WHAT IS THE FELLOWSHIP OF THE MYSTERY THAT FROM THE BEGINNING OF THE WORLD HATH BEEN HID IN GOD WHO CREATED ALL THINGS BY JESUS CHRIST."

GOD CREATED MAN IN HIS IMAGE TO HAVE A LOVING RELATIONSHIP WITH HIM.
GENESIS 1:27 "SO GOD CREATED MAN IN HIS OWN IMAGE."
GENESIS 2:7 "AND THE LORD GOD FORMED MAN OF THE DUST OF THE GROUND AND BREATHED INTO HIS NOSTRILS THE BREATH OF LIFE AND MAN BECAME A LIVING SOUL."
REVELATION 4:11 "THOU ART WORTHY O LORD TO RECEIVE GLORY AND HONOR AND POWER: FOR THOU HAST CREATED ALL THINGS AND FOR THY PLEASURE THEY ARE AND WERE CREATED."

Oh No!

GOD ³

THE BIGGEST PROBLEM BETWEEN GOD AND MAN IS SIN.
ISAIAH 59:2 "BUT THERE IS A PROBLEM YOUR SINS HAVE CUT YOU OFF FROM GOD"

MAN THEN DISOBEYED GOD AND SIN ENTERED O INTO THE WORLD. MAN FELL FROM HIS PREVIOUS POSITION AND BECAME A SINFUL BEING.
ROMANS 3:23 "FOR ALL HAVE SINNED AND COME SHORT OF THE GLORY OF GOD"
ROMANS 5:12 "THEREFORE JUST AS SIN ENTERED THE WORLD THROUGH ONE MAN AND DEATH THROUGH SIN AND THIS WAY DEATH CAME TO ALL MEN BECAUSE ALL SINNED"

THIS SEPERATION FROM GOD ONLY LEADS TO DEATH AND CERTAIN JUDGMENT.
HEBREWS 9:27 "AND FOR AS MUCH AS IT IS THE PORTION OF MEN ONCE TO DIE AND AFTER THIS JUDGMENT"

JESUS CHRIST LORD SAVE ME

GOD ⁴

HELP ME!

MATTHEW 14:13 PETER SAYS WHEN SPEAKING TO JESUS "LORD SAVE ME"

REVELATION 20:15 "WHOSOEVER WAS NOT FOUND WRITTEN IN THE BOOK OF LIFE WAS CAST INTO THE LAKE OF FIRE."

THOSE WHO DO NOT KNOW GOD AS THEIR SAVIOR WILL BE PUNISHED
2 THESSALONIANS 1:8+9 "IN FLAMING FIRE TAKING VENGEANCE ON THEM THAT KNOW NOT GOD AND THAT OBEY NOT THE GOSPEL OF OUR LORD JESUS CHRIST: WHO SHALL BE PUNISHED WITH EVERLASTING DESTRUCTION FROM THE PRESENCE OF THE LORD AND FROM THE GLORY OF HIS POWER"

SALVATION CAN NOT BE ATTAINED BY THE WORKS OF MAN OR BY LIVING A GOOD LIFE.
SALVATION IS NOT ACHIEVED BY HAVING GOOD MANNERS, BEING RELIGIOUS, INNOCENT, ETC...
EPHESIANS 2:8+9+10 "FOR IT IS BY GRACE YOU HAVE BEEN SAVED THROUGH FAITH AND THIS IS NOT FROM YOURSELVES IT IS THE GIFT OF GOD NOT BY WORKS SO THAT NO ONE CAN BOAST. FOR WE ARE GOD'S WORKMANSHIP CREATED IN CHRIST JESUS TO DO GOOD WORKS"

JESUS CHRIST LORD SAVE ME

5

GOD

EPHESIANS 2:13 "BUT NOW IN CHRIST JESUS YOU WHO ONCE WERE FAR AWAY HAVE BEEN BROUGHT NEAR THROUGH THE BLOOD OF CHRIST."

YOU MUST REPENT OF ALL YOUR SINS. ACTS 3:19 "REPENT THEN AND TURN TO GOD SO THAT YOUR SINS MAY BE WIPED OUT" ACTS 2:38 "PETER SAID UNTO THEM REPENT AND BE BAPTIZED EVERY ONE OF YOU IN THE NAME OF JESUS CHRIST FOR THE REMISSION OF SINS AND YE SHALL RECEIVE THE GIFT REPENT OF THE HOLY GHOST."

GOD LOVES YOU.

JOHN 3:16 "FOR GOD SO LOVED THE WORLD THAT HE GAVE HIS ONLY BEGOTTEN SON THAT WHOSOEVER BELIEVETH IN HIM SHOULD NOT PERISH BUT HAVE EVERLASTING LIFE." JOHN 1:12 "BUT AS MANY AS RECEIVED HIM TO THEM GAVE HE THE POWER TO BECOME THE SONS OF GOD EVEN TO THEM THAT BELIEVE IN HIS NAME"

YOU ARE SAVED BY GRACE THROUGH FAITH. FAITH IS TRUSTING IN JESUS CHRIST. EPHESIANS 2:8+9 "FOR IT IS BY GRACE THAT YOU HAVE BEEN SAVED THROUGH FAITH AND THAT NOT OF YOURSELVES; IT IS THE GIFT OF GOD; NOT OF WORKS, LEST ANY MAN SHOULD BOAST. FOR WE ARE HIS WORKMANSHIP CREATED IN CHRIST JESUS TO DO GOOD WORKS THAT GOD HAS ALREADY PREPARED" 1 JOHN 1:7 "IF WE WALK IN THE LIGHT... THE BLOOD OF JESUS CHRIST CLEANSES US FROM ALL SIN. "

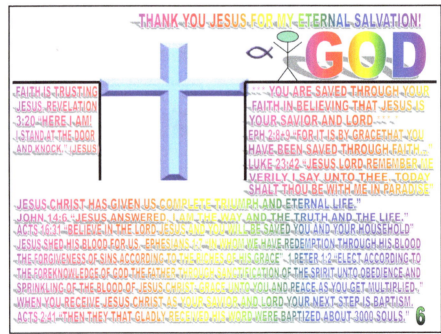

THANK YOU JESUS FOR MY ETERNAL SALVATION!

GOD

FAITH IS TRUSTING JESUS. REVELATION 3:20 "HERE I AM! I STAND AT THE DOOR AND KNOCK." (JESUS)

*** YOU ARE SAVED THROUGH YOUR FAITH IN BELIEVING THAT JESUS IS YOUR SAVIOR AND LORD *** EPH 2:8+9 "FOR IT IS BY GRACE THAT YOU HAVE BEEN SAVED THROUGH FAITH..." LUKE 23:42 "JESUS LORD REMEMBER ME VERILY I SAY UNTO THEE, TODAY SHALT THOU BE WITH ME IN PARADISE"

JESUS CHRIST HAS GIVEN US COMPLETE TRIUMPH AND ETERNAL LIFE." JOHN 14:6 "JESUS ANSWERED, I AM THE WAY AND THE TRUTH AND THE LIFE." ACTS 16:31 "BELIEVE IN THE LORD JESUS AND YOU WILL BE SAVED YOU AND YOUR HOUSEHOLD" JESUS SHED HIS BLOOD FOR US. EPHESIANS 1:7 "IN WHOM WE HAVE REDEMPTION THROUGH HIS BLOOD THE FORGIVENESS OF SINS ACCORDING TO THE RICHES OF HIS GRACE" 1 PETER 1:2 "ELECT ACCORDING TO THE FOREKNOWLEDGE OF GOD THE FATHER THROUGH SANCTIFICATION OF THE SPIRIT UNTO OBEDIENCE AND SPRINKLING OF THE BLOOD OF JESUS CHRIST. GRACE UNTO YOU AND PEACE AS YOU GET MULTIPLIED. " WHEN YOU RECEIVE JESUS CHRIST AS YOUR SAVIOR AND LORD YOUR NEXT STEP IS BAPTISM. ACTS 2:41 "THEN THEY THAT GLADLY RECEIVED HIS WORD WERE BAPTIZED ABOUT 3000 SOULS. "

6

BIRTH CERTIFICATE

7

PRAYER OF SALVATION (PRAY OUT LOUD)

DEAR JESUS I KNOW THAT I HAVE SINNED AND REPENT RIGHT NOW AND ASK YOU TO FORGIVE ME AND CLEANSE ME OF ALL MY SINS. JESUS I GIVE YOU MY LIFE AND ASK YOU TO COME INTO MY HEART AS MY SAVIOR AND LORD. NOW I KNOW THAT I HAVE ETERNAL LIFE IN HEAVEN BECAUSE YOU HAVE SAVED ME FROM THE PENALTY OF SIN. I THANK YOU JESUS CHRIST FOR THE BLOOD YOU GAVE FOR ME AT THE CROSS OF CALVARY. I ACCEPT ALL THE BLESSINGS OF YOUR PERFECT LIFE ON ALL THIS EARTH AND ALSO INTO MY LIFE AND ETERNAL SPIRIT. I NOW RECIEVE MY PLACE AS YOUR CHILD ON THIS EARTH AND FOREVER IN HEAVEN. THANK YOU JESUS FOR BEING MY SAVIOR AND LORD AND GIVING ME ETERNAL LIFE IN HEAVEN FOR ALL ETERNITY... AMEN.

SIGN _____ DATE _____

Your Next Step After Receiving Jesus Christ As Your Savior And LORD is Baptism At A Good Christian Church (Catholic, Baptist, Lutheran, Pentecostal, Etc...)

Acts 2:41 "Then they that gladly received his word were baptized: and the same day there were added unto them about 3,000 souls" Psalm 78:1 "Let my mouth be filled with thy praise" Psalm 122:1 "I was glad when they said unto me, Let us go into The House of The LORD."

YOU NOW HAVE ETERNAL LIFE IN HEAVEN AND ARE IN THE FAMILY OF GOD FOREVER!!! THE ANGELS OF HEAVEN ARE REJOICING BECAUSE YOU ARE GOING TO HEAVEN! YOU NOW HAVE ETERNAL LIFE IN HEAVEN BECAUSE YOU HAVE REPENTED OF SIN AND ACCEPTED JESUS AS YOUR SAVIOR AND LORD! JESUS SAYS LUKE 15:10 "I TELL YOU THERE IS A REJOICING IN THE PRESENCE OF THE ANGELS OF GOD OVER ONE SINNER WHO REPENTS." NOW READ THE BOOK OF JOHN... ACTS 2:21 "WHOSOEVER SHALL CALL UPON THE NAME OF THE LORD SHALL BE SAVED." JESUS CHRIST IS NOW YOUR SAVIOR!!! THIS IS THE CORRECT ANSWER! THE MAIN REASON YOU ARE SAVED AND GOING TO HEAVEN IS BECAUSE JESUS IS NOW YOUR SAVIOR AND LORD!!! YOU HAVE HAPPINESS IN HEAVEN FOREVER!

8

www.ingramcontent.com/pod-product-compliance
Lightning Source LLC
Chambersburg PA
CBHW080425060326
40689CB00019B/4386